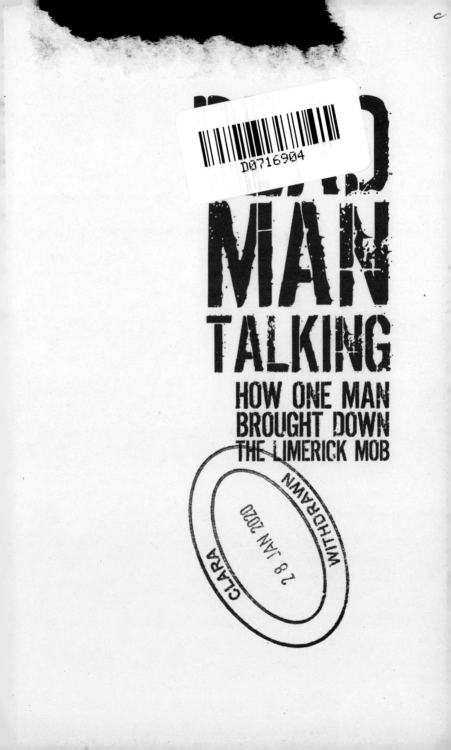

MAN
TALKING

HOW ONE MAN
BROUGHT DOWN
THE LIMERICK MOB

DEAD MAN TALKING

HOW ONE MAN BROUGHT DOWN THE LIMERICK MOB

MARK HEFFERNAN

with DARREN BOYLE

This edition published in 2012 by
Y Books
Lucan, Co. Dublin, Ireland
Tel/fax: +353 1 6217992
publishing@ybooks.ie
www.ybooks.ie

Text © 2012 Mark Heffernan and Darren Boyle
Editing, design and layout © 2012 Y Books

Paperback   ISBN: 978-1-908023-44-5
Ebook – Mobi format ISBN: 978-1-908023-45-2
Ebook – ePub format ISBN: 978-1-908023-46-9

A CIP catalogue record for this book is available from the British Library.

10 9 8 7 6 5 4 3 2 1

Typeset by Y Books
Cover design by Graham Thew Design
Cover image: www.bigstock.com
Printed and bound by CPI Cox & Wyman, Reading, Britain

DEDICATION

To the innocent victims of gang crime in Limerick

CONTENTS

ACKNOWLEDGEMENTS

MARK HEFFERNAN

I'd like to thank Darren Boyle for all the time and effort he put into helping me write this book. Thanks to Donal MacIntyre who gave me the confidence to come out of the shadows and who introduced me to Y Books. To my publisher, Chenile Keogh, and my editor, Robert Doran, who believed my story needed to be told.

To everyone involved in Changing Lives and Hill Celtic AFC, thank you for the dedication and commitment to building a brighter future for the youth of Southill.

I'd like to thank all my friends and neighbours who have stuck with me through the hard times; you know who you are.

Special thanks to Mam, Dad and my sister, Lorna, who always supported me no matter how difficult things became.

Most of all I would like to thank my partner, Gina, and our two sons, Lee and Alex, who make life worth living.

DARREN BOYLE

To Mary, Eddie, Margaret, Bridget, Eileen, JP and his parents, thank you for all your support. Thanks also to Robert Doran and Chenile Keogh at Y books, whose patience and attention made this book possible.

Lastly and most importantly, special thanks to Mark, whose inspirational story had to be told.

❖ ❖ ❖

PROLOGUE

17 FEBRUARY 2010

It was just after lunchtime when I pulled up outside the post office in Garryowen. It's on a busy street, just around the corner from the Milk Market, where my father has his market stall. The road is narrow so I parked the jeep up on the pavement to allow other traffic to pass. I was afraid to park any distance from the post office or in a car park: it just wasn't safe for me to do that any more. There were people queuing up outside, waiting for the shutters to be pulled up, so I sat behind the wheel, hoping I wouldn't have to wait too long. I'm lucky I decided to stay in the jeep. Had I joined the queue or had the post office been open, it's unlikely I'd be around to tell this story. I wouldn't have spotted the gang when they pulled up, and my next appointment would probably have been with the State Pathologist, down some lonely laneway on the Limerick/Clare border. When I worked on the club scene I met plenty of celebrities, but Marie Cassidy is one household name I have no interest in meeting.

For over a year I had been constantly on my guard, always looking over my shoulder. There are many people in Limerick who are no longer with us because they became lazy or ignored a warning. I was determined not to join them. I only ever used the back roads these days, to dodge traffic and avoid being seen. I couldn't keep a regular routine and would never bring my children to school. The gangs have plenty of pennyboys who act as runners, couriers and spotters. It wouldn't take long for a tip-off to reach the gang, and once they knew where to find me, I could be guaranteed they would waste no time doing exactly that.

As I sat in my Toyota Land Cruiser, waiting for the post office to reopen after lunch, I kept the engine ticking over. I noticed that the low-fuel light was on and made a mental note to get diesel after I had finished my business in the post office. Around about then a blue Volvo pulled up beside me, with Gareth Collins behind the wheel. Collins is one of the hard-men in the McCarthy/Dundon gang. I immediately noticed that he was wearing a pair of black gloves. This is never a good sign. It may have been February, but I don't think he was wearing gloves to keep his hands warm. Sitting beside him in the passenger's seat was Ger Dundon. That was worse again. Ger has a big house out on the Hyde Road next to his brother Wayne's and he never seems to be short of cash despite not having a job. The dogs on the street know he's a gangster, but nobody would dare to give evidence in court. To stand up to the McCarthy/Dundons is to sign your own death warrant. In the back of the car I saw the two Skull McGintys and a third person I didn't recognise.

As soon as the Volvo came to a halt, the back doors flew open and the two Skull McGintys jumped out and ran towards my jeep. They were coming for me and they didn't look like they were going to invite me for tea and biscuits. I knew something was wrong so I threw the Land Cruiser into gear and drove off. There were plenty of witnesses outside the post office but I knew that people who would salute you every day on the street would suddenly forget they had seen you, when the guards called round. They might feel sorry for you and sympathise with your family, but they know if they step forward, they'll be the next person in the firing line, and you couldn't blame them for keeping quiet.

As I headed up the road, there was a car coming straight for me, blocking my escape route, and I was forced to turn right even though I knew I was driving into a dead end. I tried not to panic; if I lost the head I was finished. I accelerated down to the bottom of the cul-de-sac, swung the jeep around and reversed a small bit to give myself a little more breathing space. I was gripping the steering wheel hard. The adrenaline was pumping and my heart was beating out of my chest. I certainly felt alive – and I wanted to keep it that way. The jeep was in gear, ready to go. I just needed a little time to work out a plan. It was like something out of a movie, but it was very real.

Collins stopped his Volvo at the end of the road, blocking the only exit from the cul-de-sac. The McGintys and Dundon jumped out and ran towards me. Meanwhile Collins walked around to the back of the Volvo and opened the boot. He stood there and watched as the others advanced on me, certain they had blocked my escape route. Dundon was waving his hands at me. One of the McGintys had an iron bar in his fist and the other had a hammer.

They were seconds away from me and I was running out of time. Their car was blocking the road, but there was still a little space on the footpath. I didn't know if the jeep would fit through the gap

but it was my only chance of escape. I put my foot
to the floor and heard the tyres screech as the jeep
leapt forward.

Ger Dundon and the two McGintys were right
in front of me. They got out of the way just in
time, jumping over a wall and into someone's front
garden. There was no way I was stopping, and at
that point I was prepared to mow them over if I had
to. It was kill or be killed.

I got the jeep up to a good speed and pulled it up
on the footpath. I set my sights on the gap and prayed
to God I'd fit through. I made it with a couple of
inches to spare and sped out onto the street. Luckily
there was no oncoming traffic, so I turned right.
Going the other way would have brought me back
into the centre of the city and I couldn't risk getting
stuck in traffic. I was thinking as fast as I could,
trying to figure out a way to safety. I decided to
drive through the heart of Keane/Collopy territory.
I reckoned the McCarthy/Dundons might not risk
entering their arch-rivals' turf. I flew past the
Garryowen shrine, with Kieran Keane's house on
my right, hoping that they didn't want me enough to
risk their own lives. But when I looked in the rear-
view mirror I saw the blue Volvo, still coming after
me. It looked like they were determined. I quickly
glanced at the dashboard, where the orange low-fuel

light was shining brightly. The jeep was running on fumes now. I needed help – quickly.

I picked up my phone but I fumbled, trying to unlock it, and it slipped out of my hand and fell into the passenger foot well. I needed to get to Roxboro Road Garda Station but I knew that if I turned right out of Garryowen, I'd get caught in traffic, so my only option was to head out the Dublin Road and take a longer route that would allow me to keep moving. I knew that if I stopped I was a dead man. When I got to St Patrick's Road, near the Parkville Court Hotel, there was a line of cars ahead of me and the traffic lights were red. I pulled into the middle of the road, dropped down a gear and floored it. The Volvo was gaining on me, so I had to tear down the white line and break the red light. This wasn't the time to be worrying about penalty points. The other drivers must have thought I was crazy. I sped past at least fifteen cars, hoping a pedestrian wouldn't step into my path and end up under the jeep. I knew I was endangering lives but I was in fear for my own. The diesel situation was getting critical. I was playing fuel-light lottery with my life, and I was trying to fish my mobile phone up from the floor without killing myself or anyone else.

As I was approaching the Parkway Shopping Centre, the traffic started backing up again. I swung onto the wrong side of the road and steered straight for the roundabout. I powered up over the kerb and across the grass, hopping off the far side of the roundabout, trying to save every possible second. I knew the Volvo wouldn't get over the roundabout and it might give me some small advantage. Every metre I put between us increased the chance of my survival. I took the road that led past T.K. Maxx and Homebase, where there were no traffic lights and little chance of traffic.

I finally managed to grab my phone and call the guards. I was continually changing gear to get every ounce of power from the jeep, and it was very tricky to talk on the phone, steer and stay in the right gear, while keeping an eye on the Volvo behind me at the same time.

I told the guards exactly who was in the Volvo so they knew it was serious. I was heading towards the Groody Road and I warned them that I was then going to head across to the Ballysimon Road. It was all clear in my mind at that stage. I needed them to intercept the Volvo before I ran out of fuel and was left stranded like a sitting duck. All I had to do was keep going and hope I had enough diesel to last me.

The buildings gave way to trees and fields as I headed out of the city. I was trying to lead them on a loop around the outskirts of Limerick, hoping that

the gardaí could lay a trap for them. It was a bit of a
risk, but I was gunning it hard, keeping up a speed
of 120 km/h and I didn't think they could catch me
as long as I had fuel. But when I glanced in the
rear-view mirror, they were closing in on me. My
heart was pounding and sweat was dripping down
my face. I was trying not to lose control and end up
ploughing into a tree. No matter how fast I went, I
couldn't lose them.

At the next roundabout I wanted to go right.
Instead of keeping to my lane like you would in
your driving test, I cut the corner and sped through
the roundabout, narrowly missing a car. I had no
other option as the Volvo was right behind me now.
I dropped down a couple of gears and the tyres
struggled for a grip on the tarmac. The jeep was
rolling like a ship on a stormy sea as I slammed
my foot hard on the throttle, listening to the turbo
whine before quickly changing up a gear to keep the
power coming. I felt like the Stig doing a flying lap
on *Top Gear*, only I was driving for my life.

About thirty seconds later I heard sirens. I looked
in the rear-view mirror and saw the first squad cars
catch up with the Volvo. The guards pulled Collins
over but I could only see uniformed officers and
I knew that they wouldn't be carrying guns. The
McCarthy/Dundon gang have no respect for the

gardaí and they could easily have made a call for reinforcements of their own. I knew there could be a second car full of gang members on the way. There was no way I was stopping until I felt safe. I continued up the middle of the road, straddling the white line. The fact that they had followed me that distance, and through Keane/Collopy territory too, proved they really wanted me, so I wasn't going to relax and make a mistake when I was nearly home and dry.

It wasn't until I drove into the car park of Roxboro Road Garda Station and walked through the front door that I breathed a sigh of relief. I was happy that the lads had been arrested and the nightmare that I had been living for the past twelve months would now be over. Little did I know that the fun was only starting.

❖ ❖ ❖

ONE

BORN SLIPPY

I grew up in Carew Park, in Southill on the southside of Limerick City. It's a local authority estate made up of a series of terraces built during the 1960s. Over the years some of the houses have been burned out and the area has become quite rundown. Anytime Carew Park is mentioned on the news it is in relation to a shooting or the discovery of a hidden arms cache. It might not be the prettiest area in the world, but there's a strong sense of community and we've always had great neighbours and friends there. Growing up, it was just my mam and dad and my sister, Lorna, in our house and we were a happy, close-knit family.

If you asked most people on the estate who John Carew is, they would probably tell you he's

the Norwegian international striker who played for
Valencia, Aston Villa and West Ham. Some joker
even edited the footballer's entry on Wikipedia
to claim that Carew Park had been renamed in
honour of the striker, following a vote by the Villa
supporters in the area. As one of the few Villa fans
in Southill, I wish that was the case, but the truth is
sadly much more mundane. In Limerick our estates
aren't named after Irish patriots like Padraig Pearse
or Wolfe Tone, but rather former mayors of the city,
and John Carew was the Mayor of Limerick in the
1960s.

There are plenty of green spaces in Carew Park
and as a young fella I spent most of my time out
playing football. Somebody always had a football to
kick around one of the fields surrounding the estate.
We played baseball and tennis, and there was a
boxing club that kept us busy in the evenings. It was
a very energetic and sporty lifestyle. On Saturdays
we'd often head off into the countryside for a long
walk. Then when we came back to Southill, we'd go
straight over to the local hall, where the Jonesboro
Football Club used to run regular discos for us.

The discos in Southill in the early 1990s were
very tame affairs. The DJ would belt out a few
tunes, and instead of laser shows, plasma screens
and dry ice, there was a simple traffic-light rig-up.

If there was a strobe light it was considered the height of sophistication. I remember that everyone loved the Peter Andre track 'Mysterious Girl', as it was huge at the time. I cringe now every time I hear the track. It was all very innocent and simple, but it was an example of the community trying to organise events for the youngsters, and they were always good fun. Sometimes the DJ would let me have a go on the decks, which helped to spark my fascination with music and DJing.

I joined the Southill Marching Band and played the drums. It was an opportunity to hang out with girls as they were never really interested in football.

I met my first girlfriend a little closer to home, though. I was standing beside the front wall of the house, chatting with two friends, when three girls walked past. I took an immediate fancy to one of the girls and I made a bet with my mates that I was going to go out with her. I was fourteen years of age and I had all the arrogance of youth and enough self-confidence to think I could approach any girl in the world. I knew the girl from seeing her around but I didn't know her name. I didn't run after her there and then because I didn't want to look desperate. Instead I came up with a plan and engineered a meeting.

I found out that her name was Gina and that she

was from Keyes Park, which is the neighbouring estate. Gina's uncle owned a shop across from our house and I used to do a bit of part-time work there, stacking shelves and helping behind the counter. A few days later she came into the shop and I decided to make my approach. I wasn't nervous at all because I was just going to have a bit of a chit-chat with her. During the conversation I asked her if she wanted to go out sometime. She said yes and we started going to gigs and events.

I remember one day when I was visiting Gina's house, her father tried to catch me out. He asked me, 'If you had to leave Limerick tomorrow, how much money could you get together?' It wasn't a serious question, so I looked at him and put on a serious face. With a heavy breath I said, 'Well I guess I could get £50,000 from one of the bank accounts for starters.' I was just winding him up. It was a trick question but I think he could tell at that stage that I'd be a regular caller to his house. Even at fourteen, I was very streetwise, and working alongside my father on his market stall eliminated any shyness.

There was never any money handed over for the bet I made with my mates. I didn't need a cash incentive to approach Gina and it was probably the best decision I've made in my life. Fourteen years later we're still together and we have two beautiful children. We had great craic growing up together and we are best friends as well as everything else. We're both very easy going and are well suited to each other.

I went to Our Lady of Lourdes School in Weston, which is about two miles away from my home. My mother is from Weston and a lot of my cousins went to the same school.

It was at Our Lady's that I first met some of the members of what would later become the McCarthy/Dundon crime gang. Christopher McCormack was in the same class as me but he was never interested in football, so I didn't have a great deal to do with him. His brother David was in the class below me, and Gareth Collins, another gang member, was in the class above me. The Collins family was very well known in Limerick. Jimmy Collins, Gareth's dad, was a renowned hard man. My family never had any dealings with him, but he was well known as somebody who was not to be crossed and he commanded a lot of respect in the area.

I got into quite a few scraps with Christopher and David McCormack in the schoolyard. It was never anything very serious, just a lot of pushing and shoving. They were known as the Skull McGintys, although if you called them that to their faces they would start throwing punches. I think it was a nickname that had been given to one of their relatives and it stuck to the entire family. If you got hassled in the yard you'd just go head-to-head and face-to-face with the other kid. I wasn't exactly a shy child and I gave as good as I got. It never went too far.

We spent the school day waiting for the two breaks when we could play football. That was the highlight of our day and we even kept records of who scored the most goals each week or each month. The captains picked their players in turn and everyone prayed that he wouldn't be the last man picked, because that would make him the worst player.

After primary school I went to Crescent Comprehensive in Raheen. I was only ever really interested in woodwork, technical drawing and maths. When I was in history or English class, I'd have my drawing equipment out on the desk and I'd be completely ignoring the teacher. I regret not paying attention now, because if I had done some work I might have found it interesting.

Eventually the teachers had enough of it and I was suspended for not paying attention in class. The principal called me into his office and said he wanted to meet with my mother. This presented a very serious problem. I didn't want to do anything that would break my mother's heart, and getting suspended from school would have been a major thing. There was no way I could tell her about it and my father would have gone mental if he found out.

So the only solution was to find myself a 'surrogate' mother for the day. I paid a woman from the area a few pounds to come along with me to the school and pretend to be Mrs Heffernan. The principal had never met my mother and if I had my way, he never would. The woman agreed to it because she thought it might be fun, and she didn't have any children at Crescent Comprehensive so that wasn't a problem. I was sitting beside her as the principal began listing off my failings. He said I needed to apply myself better and pay attention in class. He said I would be welcome back to the school if I changed my ways. 'Mrs Heffernan' promised to get me to pay attention and work harder and the situation was sorted without the real Mrs Heffernan ever getting wind of it.

Of course I never factored in the fact that we would have a parent/teacher meeting a few months later. When the day rolled round, I had to bring the same woman back again because it would have seemed rather strange to return with a different mother. That's the problem with deception: once you start lying, it's difficult to stop.

I stayed in school until my Junior Cert and after that I was out the door, never to return. Leaving school early was an easy decision for me. In areas like Southill those who go on to sit the Leaving Cert are in the minority. There was no stigma attached to deciding that school was not the best option for a young fella looking to make his mark on the world. The points race and CAO offers are a million miles from the reality of life in Southill. There are those who cling on to their childhood and schooldays like a security blanket, unwilling to take the step into the big bad world. I know education is vital, but everyone has to learn their own lessons and not everyone is suited to becoming a brain surgeon.

Around the time of the Junior Cert, my woodwork teacher said to me, 'Mark, why are you still in school when you could be out there earning money?' He said there was no point in me staying in school for another three years when I could be doing a carpentry course. It was an appealing idea. By the time the rest of my class would be doing their Leaving Cert, I could be a fully qualified carpenter. It gave me something to aim for and I decided to take his advice.

I ditched the schoolbag and replaced it with a hammer and chisel. My uncle was a carpenter so I knew what the work entailed, and a strong work ethic had been drummed into us from a very young age. My father was always busy, whether he was driving a coal lorry, delivering fuel across the city, or selling goods from his market stall. He showed me the value of work and how to make a pound. He has been a major influence on my life and he got behind me when I decided to become a carpenter.

I signed up with FÁS to train as a carpenter. I was learning about working with wood but it was still too much like school for me, sitting in a classroom all day long. I stuck with the course, though, because I needed the qualification and under the scheme there was some time allocated for working on site. For me, that's where the real learning began.

I started working with Martin Fitzgibbon Builders through a contact of my father's. Building came naturally to me. I was always a great man for the Lego when I was growing up; I'd just pick up the blocks, look at the picture and build whatever was on the box. I spent a lot of time doing snag lists and bits and pieces, finishing off the houses. I was getting real experience, learning on the job, which is what it's all about.

Before long I was making more money doing nixers than I was on the FÁS course.

I was doing my own job, but then I was getting extra work because I knew what I was doing and

I was always willing to do it. An apprentice is normally expected to do all the menial jobs like lifting bales of wood and or carrying things on your shoulder. I missed out on all of that. I never did the donkey work.

The foreman would often be working between two sites, and when he went away he would call me over and ask me to keep an eye on things. I guess he knew he could trust me. There were a lot of houses in the area being refurbished and often people would want extra bits of work done outside the terms of the contract. They would hire the foreman direct and he would split the profits with me on any bit of work I had done. I was building extensions before I was seventeen. I finished my first one before I had even completed the FÁS course.

I definitely preferred being on site to being in the classroom at the FÁS training centre in Raheen. They'd teach you how to do something one way in the classroom but on site it was often completely different.

I was enjoying the carpentry work, but I was really getting into music too. Because I was earning good money for a young fella and I didn't waste it on drink or drugs, I could afford to buy some DJing equipment, like a CD mixing desk. The money I was earning on the sites allowed me to develop my

interest in music to the point where it was becoming
my main focus.

In a way I think I'm lucky I started working at such
a young age. It gave me something to concentrate
on and kept me on the straight and narrow. Some of
the kids I went to school with are now completely
destroyed by drugs. Hash was the most popular
drug when I was a young lad. Hash and Scrumpy
Jack cider were the big things. The fellas would get
an adult to buy a few flagons for them and they'd
head down to the park to get wasted and boast about
imaginary experiences with girls.

It didn't take long for some of the guys to start
experimenting with speed, cocaine, ecstasy and
then, for the really unlucky ones, heroin. Most drugs
were easy to get hold of. The gangs would hand
out free samples to get as many people as possible
hooked. Everyone from the area knew who the local
dealer was; it was as easy as buying an apple.

When I left school I was determined that I wasn't
going to spend my life hanging around the fields,
drinking cider by the flagon. I look around me and
see those people and think, *Thank God I didn't go
that route.*

Heroin is an absolute killer. It wrecks lives and
not just those of the addicts. Guys I knew in school
are now mere shells, just zombies on the hunt for

their next fix, not caring who they hurt to get it.

Drugs always lead to crime and my own family has experience of this. When I was about twelve, I was at home with my father and sister one evening, around 10 p.m. My mother was out at work and she was due home around that time. So when there was a knock at the door, I ran into the hall and turned the lock to let my mam in. Three men wearing balaclavas burst into the house. Two of them were carrying sawn-off shotguns. They forced their way into the living room and one of them pointed his gun at me. The leader shouted at my father and told him to hand over any cash he had in the house or he would start shooting.

My father was known to have a bit of cash from the few businesses he was involved in. He wasn't a millionaire or anything but he always had a bit of money.

It all happened very quickly and I was in shock. All I could see was the barrel of the gun pointing at me, and the eyes of the gunman. I knew from the raiders' accents that they were from Limerick but I didn't know who they were. I don't think they were from Southill. My dad was delivering coal all over the city so they could have been from another part of Limerick.

Dad remained calm; he didn't get angry or look

scared. He handed over about £500 that he had in the house and the raiders made their escape.

Having three men hold us up in the house was a life changing experience. It did not make me afraid of living in Carew Park but I was wary of answering the front door after that. Before the raid, I would run out and open the front door when someone called, without thinking. Afterwards I had to know who was there. I guess that was a part of the end of innocence. Somebody had invaded the safety of our home and a wariness has stayed with me ever since.

❖ ❖ ❖

TWO

RADIO GA GA

Working on building sites can be incredibly satisfying. The fruit of your day's work is there to be seen immediately, whether it's the drying section of a wall or a newly hung door. You get a real sense of progress. There is even a certain buzz to be had when you walk by a job you completed years before and see the walls still standing. Sometimes small things can make a massive difference when you are working on sites and I learned that it is attention to detail that often bridges the gap between success and failure or between an acceptable job and an outstanding one. If you immerse yourself in something and study every detail, you are far more likely to succeed.

That's the attitude I took when it came to music.

Music has always been very important to me and I was desperate for it to be more than just a pastime. Ever since I had played with the Southside Marching Band, I had enjoyed performing in public and I really wanted to make a living from it.

Every evening when I got home from work, I'd lock myself away in the bedroom and take out the CD decks. I spent hours teaching myself how to mix tracks together and developing a feel for why certain tracks work well with each other. It was very hit and miss and I was very raw in the beginning, but I persevered and gradually I got better. At the end of every week when I got paid, I would invest in new equipment and gadgets that would help me hone my skills. These were the days before illegal downloading and high-speed broadband, and I spent a fortune building my CD collection.

My family knew about my interest in music and one afternoon my cousin approached me and asked if I would DJ at his baby's christening. It was to be held in the Haven Pub, just off Parnell Street in Limerick City Centre. This wasn't some tiny church hall – it was a real venue. It was a massive step up from sitting in my bedroom with headphones, pretending I was DJing in front of 200 people. The fact that most of the crowd were related to me didn't matter, and I didn't care that I wouldn't be paid for the gig – I was just excited to be getting the experience.

My imagination was soon running wild and I had visions of working the decks at an exclusive Monte Carlo nightclub with a string of super models on the dance floor, telling Bono that he had to buy a ticket like everyone else.

The gig went exceptionally well; the dance floor was rarely empty and the crowd seemed to really enjoy themselves. It was a great boost to my confidence and it even got me started in business. as some of the guests asked my cousin for my phone number because they wanted me to DJ at their parties.

In 1999 Tony Calvert was the main man on the Limerick DJ scene. He organised all the entertainment for Steve Collins, who owned Brannigan's and The Steering Wheel – two of the most popular bars in the city. Steve's family had recently returned from Blackpool in the UK, where they had run a highly successful nightclub.

I was introduced to Tony, who had heard that I was an ambitious young DJ. We hit it off immediately. He was like a walking music encyclopaedia and his home was stacked full of more CDs and vinyl than I'd ever seen in my life. He must be the only man in the mid-west who thought the 10,000-track capacity of the iPod was a bit small.

Tony was like a musical Yoda passing on his knowledge to his young Jedi apprentice. There is far more to being a DJ than just putting a CD in the machine and pressing play. The DJ's job is not just to play music; it is to give the crowd a great time using the right music for the right occasion. It's the crowd who create the atmosphere after it has been teased out of them by the music.

Tony opened my mind to different styles of music and revealed that there were excellent tracks recorded before 1996! I knew nothing of the 1960s, 70s or 80s. He introduced me to all the best one-hit wonders and essential tracks. He could tell you which obscure track to throw on in the middle of a party to make the entire place explode. The wrong tune can kill the buzz quicker than the local sergeant raiding a nightclub, so a good DJ has to be able to read the audience to see what type of music they are going to respond to.

I'd never go to a gig with a playlist. Thanks to Tony, no matter what crowd you put in front of me, I'd know what to play for them. The trick is to play music people recognise, but not the chart music that is constantly on the radio. You need to drop in the odd one-hit-wonder and then hit them with a massive floor filler.

Mark Rooney was another DJ who was well established on the local scene. I spent hours hanging around with him at gigs, helping him carry the equipment, all the while observing and learning as much as I could. Philip Scanlan and his friend Kieran Judge also helped me out a lot and often lent me equipment such as an amp or some lights while I was saving to buy my own.

I was still only sixteen but I was becoming far more professional in my approach. I had a couple of regular gigs and was making my name on the scene when Tony made the proverbial offer you couldn't refuse. He said he would sell me all his DJ equipment and set me up with his regular gigs across the city. That was incredibly generous of Tony as it was a profitable business. It was definitely moving things up to the next level and I accepted the offer without even thinking about it.

My main problem now was transport. I bought a two-year-old, blue Toyota Hiace van to carry all my DJ equipment. A popular show on MTV at the time was *Pimp My Ride,* in which rapper XZibit customised some deserving person's car. That gave me the idea to pimp my van and, luckily, I could employ my carpentry skills to line the inside with plywood. Then I fitted carpet to the floor, walls and roof to stop the gear bouncing around the rear of

the van. Like on the show, the main feature was
the ICE – the in-car entertainment – and Limerick's
own passion wagon could give the finest American
creations a run for their money on that score.

Now the only thing holding me back was my age.
I had to wait until I was seventeen before I could
legally get behind the wheel. Eventually, with the
seventeen candles on the cake blown out and that
little green piece of card in my back pocket, I was
unstoppable.

For some the entertainment business is a sideline
or a handy nixer, but I saw huge potential in it. The
Celtic Tiger was beginning to roar and people had
plenty of money to spend on entertainment. At
the same time technology was rapidly improving,
with the introduction of plasma screens, lasers and
digital mixing decks. Now a guy working from the
back of a Hiace van could put on a show that five
years previously would have been impossible for a
DJ in a top London club.

My plan was to blow the competition out of the
water by investing in the best equipment, and it was
working. The bookings were coming in hard and
fast it was almost impossible to keep up. I always
had a young lad with me to give me a hand, much in
the same way I had helped Tony Calvert and Mark
Rooney. The young fellas were dying to learn the

tricks, and once they were ready I'd set them up with their own night and build the business that way.

In early 2000 the scene was developing and Karaoke was becoming very popular, with wannabe Whitney Houstons declaring their undying love night after night. The main problem with Karaoke is the time it takes to start the next song once the previous one has ended. It can get messy when a DJ calls Mary from the back of the bar to sing 'A Woman's Heart' and there's no music playing for several minutes while she is persuaded to take to the stage. Even though Mary is dying to sing the song, she still needs encouragement to get up there. That might be great craic for Mary and her friends but the rest of the bar gets bored with it very quickly.

Disco Karaoke was the way forward. As soon as a song finished I had music ready immediately, so there was no gap in the entertainment. This gave plenty of time for the reluctant star to come up on stage. Little details like this gave us the edge over other Karaoke nights.

Another problem with Karaoke is that some people simply cannot sing. The odd tuneless rendition of 'I Will Survive' will have the crowd laughing, but a string of talentless singers will soon get them annoyed. My solution to this came in the form of one Emma O'Driscoll. Emma is a wonderful singer and people would come specifically to hear her perform. At one stage, Emma, her aunt and her sister were all singing for me and they never failed to impress the audience. Soon afterwards, Emma won the RTÉ *Popstars* show as part of the band Six, who were managed by Louis Walsh for a time. Bringing Emma and her family into the show made it look far more professional and it meant that people would endure the bad performers because they knew the girls would put on a great show.

The hard work was paying off. By 2001 I had between eight and ten DJs operating every Saturday night. Things were getting very hectic. After breakfast there was always a mad race around the city to deliver equipment to the various venues, set it up and perform a sound check, before returning home for a quick dinner. Some of the younger DJs needed a lift to their venues and then I would go off to do my own gig. After closing time I had to collect all the gear and drop off everyone, before heading home to bed at around 5 a.m.

One night I was dropping off one of the staff at their house in St Mary's Park. The area is known locally as the Island and is home to the Keane/ Collopy gang. It has one road in and one road out. Unfortunately for the paintwork of the passion wagon, someone driving a similar blue Hiace had been showing an unhealthy interest in the girlfriend of a leading gang member. This prompted the local kids to pick up bricks, bottles and anything else that was to hand and pelt their missiles at the van. It sounded like a monster hailstorm. I had no idea why they were attacking. There was €10,000 worth of kit in the back but it didn't seem like a hijacking. I quickly dropped off my friend and sped for the exit, thinking myself lucky to have escaped without injury.

The following morning I got a call from one of the senior gang members. He apologised and told me it was a case of mistaken identity and said if I came back to the Island he would sort out the damage. As I was leaving with the cash to pay for the repairs in my pocket, he said, 'Mark, you're a lucky man. One of the young fellas went off to get the gun and he couldn't find it.'

I took things to another level when I introduced Lionel Vinyl to the scene. Lionel first appeared in Blackpool in the UK and I thought the character would work brilliantly in Limerick. The outfit consisted of a giant Afro wig, gold medallions and a flared tiger-skin suit. There was so much static electricity in the air from the man-made fibres that you could have powered the entire kit from it.

Lionel Vinyl made his debut in Brannigan's in 2001 and he was an instant hit. People couldn't get enough of him. He had two beautiful sidekicks, K-Tel and Poly-Ester, who handed him CDs and entertained the crowd with their disco moves. Lionel took to the stage with a confident swagger, his chest thrust forward like a cartoon rooster. He spoke directly to the crowd and got them to put their hands in the air, before giving them some basic instructions on the art of disco dancing. The crowd loved Lionel and many joined in the fun and dressed up in vintage gear too. It was a licence to act silly and get the audience hyped up. It was so simple but it was genius.

They key was that I had no shame. Getting dressed up like a pimp from *Dirty Harry* didn't bother me in the slightest. It was all about entertaining the crowd and it worked – that was all that mattered.

Before long, I was the biggest player on the DJ scene in Limerick. I had it all sewn up. My organisation was so big that by the time I was eighteen, if someone booked an event in a bar in Limerick, it would most likely be one of my DJs supplying the music. We offered guarantees that everything would work like clockwork, and that meant we could charge top dollar. We raised the bar in terms of what was being provided. Other DJs were using old equipment, while mine was state of the art and absolutely reliable. Instead of old-fashioned disco lights I was using giant flat-screen monitors and lasers. It was like a DJ arms race.

The disco scene was ticking over very nicely and I was making a tidy profit. Lionel Vinyl's Boogie Wonderland was a massive success and everyone was doing well out of it. It was then that a highly unusual proposition was made to me.

One evening I was doing a gig in the Sallyport and Donald Crawford came up to me and presented me with his business card. He said he was working for Kiss FM and that he would like me to come in and meet them. Kiss FM was the biggest pirate station in Limerick at the time. It was massive. They wanted to talk to me about doing my own show, which was great for my ego as it meant I was getting noticed for doing a good job.

I thought about it for a few days and then I called Donald and said I'd give it a go. I had nothing to lose by giving it a shot.

A pirate radio station is an illegal operation, so you can't have a sign outside advertising its presence. Donald said he would pick me up and bring me to the station. I didn't know what to expect, but when I walked into the building I was quietly impressed.

They had a great set-up, with modern professional equipment. That seemed strange because the place could be raided by the Broadcasting Commission of Ireland (BCI) at any time, and all the equipment seized.

I saw working on Kiss FM as a great opportunity as it reached almost every home in Limerick. This was great exposure for the disco and club nights and it helped to build my profile.

Soon after I joined the station it became clear that it was struggling financially. The owners were having a few problems and they were looking to sell. I could see that there was potential in pirate radio but I thought the station needed a radical overhaul. I felt that it could be the ideal advertising platform because it had such a wide reach. So I decided to buy the radio station with the money I had saved from DJing. It was a big decision but I really believed that it would pay off in the long run.

The first major decision after taking over was to ditch the Kiss FM name. We decided to rebrand as Wave FM. Buying the radio station was not a vanity project; it was a serious business proposition. The previous owners of Kiss FM had started running successful teen events, which I had now inherited. I wanted to break from the old-style events and introduce spectaculars. By bringing things to the next level I felt the teenagers would arrive en-masse. The radio station was perfect for advertising the events and pulling in a big crowd.

When we were growing up the major event on the social calendar was the local disco, but they were fairly tame affairs. It was very clear that Celtic Tiger teenagers had plenty of money but there were very few events that targeted them. A properly run teenage event could be very lucrative. The most important thing was to convince the teenagers that the event was unmissable. Then you had to persuade the parents that everything was above board, safe and supervised. There was no point in selling loads of tickets only for the teenagers to be told by fearful mums and dads that they couldn't go. The key to running a successful teen event is to win the confidence of parents by convincing them that the event is well run and safe. At the time there were a lot of radio shows and newspapers reporting on teenage discos and the appalling behaviour that was allowed to go on at them. Photographs of drunken youngsters falling around were commonplace. We would constantly emphasise that the management reserved the right to refuse admission and we set up a parent information line to offer reassurance that everything was being properly run. The events were alcohol free and we made it clear to the teens that if they had drink taken, they were not going to get in. Worse still for them, we would contact their parents and report them for being drunk. We spent a fortune on security and medical support. Everything was done to the highest possible standard because one slip-up could destroy the reputation of the company. Everything was done to build our reputation – even down to something as simple as the bus tickets, which had barcodes and were fully branded with our logos. We knew that high production values would inspire confidence among the parents. We also said that neat dress was essential. We were showing the teens a great deal of respect and demanded that they did the same.

Up until we hit the scene, a teen event would be a disco in a GAA hall with a few extra lights and a couple of GAA club members manning the doors. The kids often got bored and then they would run wild, causing trouble.

We made a lot of mistakes in the early days of Wave FM but we learned from them and we learned quickly. One mistake that Pirate Radio stations often make is to sell advertising. This annoys the legitimate local station as you are essentially stealing their revenue, and they will waste no time in reporting you to the BCI. I didn't bother with advertising because it would cause problems for 95FM and the last thing we needed was to have them on our back.

Our business plan revolved entirely around the teenage events, and we could still promote those on air without annoying the competition. We consciously never called them discos because they were far more than that and we wanted to get the message across that they were something special.

The events were all branded as Wave FM nights and this created its own set of problems. We would approach a venue, pay for the rental in cash and then book our entertainment. On too many occasions the hotel owners would call me and say that people were phoning and saying it was a pirate radio station behind the event. The upshot was that the owner would cancel our event and leave us without a venue.

The solution was beautifully elegant in its simplicity. Our main problem was having a gig named after an illegal radio station. We needed all the teens to go mad about the radio station but the gigs had to be called something else so that there was no direct link between the two.

I was sharing an office with Roy Collins at the time. Roy was the son of Steve Collins, who owned Brannigan's. He was supplying jukeboxes, poker machines and fruit machines to venues around Munster, having recently returned to Limerick from Blackpool, where he had run a night in a club called Federation. We were sitting around having a chat when he pulled out a folder. Inside it he had all these flyers with the Federation logo. It only took a few seconds for him to sell the concept to me. All the artwork looked very professional so there was no point in me changing it or paying a fortune to have new design work done.

Roy said to me: 'I don't use that stuff any more; do you want it? Use it, because it saves you the hassle of coming up with a name and a logo and design work. It's all there.' So that was the name for the events sorted, and we didn't have to spend a penny on branding.

In the UK there was a satellite radio station called Galaxy FM. The station had a strong brand identity but nobody had ever heard of it in Limerick at the time. I decided to rebrand Wave FM as Galaxy and piggyback on their marketing and branding. Branding any business can be expensive. But with Galaxy, all we had to do was pay a few quid for a Sky box and record the UK promos and jingles. It was a massive station in the UK and they spent over £1 million a year on promotion. They would have people like Beyoncé on, saying, 'Hi, this is Beyoncé and you're listening to Galaxy FM.' The other stations in Limerick couldn't believe it when they heard Beyoncé promoting us!

We launched Federation and Galaxy around 2004. Galaxy FM ran ads for Federation nights but there was no connection on paper linking the companies. We had events in Doon Community Hall in County Limerick and the Two Mile Inn. There was even a special event for the over tens and under fourteens, which both proved to be massive hits. Before long we were running gigs for more than 1,000 teenagers.

Even for the junior event we were able to charge €10 a ticket. The older nights were around the €12 mark. The leaflets and flyers were very professional and we arranged for buses to bring the kids to and from the venues.

By the time we launched Galaxy FM we had even sorted out issues with the signal. The Wave FM signal was pretty weak, so we put up an aerial in Southill, the second highest point in the city. The aerial wasn't disturbed in three years of broadcasting. I had a friend who knew everything about getting a good signal and he said the higher the aerial, the better the signal. So Southill was a great location. We didn't bother trying to secure planning permission for the aerial, as Limerick County Council would have wanted to know why we wanted to erect this massive pole.

Not once did we lose a transmitter to the Broadcasting Commission. RLO – another Limerick pirate – were broadcasting at the same time as Galaxy and they were losing probably three transmitters a month because they were stepping on 95FM's toes by stealing their advertising. Meanwhile I had a massive pole transmitting from the middle of Southill and no one paid any attention.

We made our money through the gigs. The station was a hobby for most of the lads who were working there. The DJs would get paid if they were working in a pub at night, but on the radio they were doing it for free. The only people who were getting paid were the technicians and the guys looking after the aerial. At any one time I probably had a crew of twenty DJs. The lads were very enthusiastic and were willing to work for nothing just to get on the air and get some experience.

An important lesson I learned was that there could be thirty seconds of dead air between one-track ending and the next one starting, and you can't broadcast silence and expect to keep the interest of listeners. I learned how to use software called Cool Edit Pro, which allowed me to modify the jingles by changing the sound levels. The software allowed us to run seamlessly from a track to a jingle to a Federation advert to another track, and this eliminated the problem of dead air. I'd spend hours at night doing stuff like that and trying to get the music right for the station.

When we set up Galaxy, we moved into Eastway Business Park. This was a fairly major undertaking. We set up a full recording studio upstairs, where we recorded the voice-overs. It had a huge glass window so people could look in on the studio. But the main action was downstairs. This is where the live radio studio was located. The only problem with locating the live station in a fairly central location was the chance that it could be raided by the BCI. We designed the system in such a manner that a single switch could turn off the broadcast from the main studio, and this would start the back-up recording from a computer beside the transmitter in Southill. In a matter of seconds we could stop broadcasting from the studio and we would no longer be breaking the law. The back-up system ensured that the station remained on the air unless the BCI located the actual transmitter. We could claim that because there was no transmitter to be found, the studio was only a sound production facility. Although the BCI could use specialised equipment to home in on the signal and trace it back to its source, they had to catch you in the act.

No one outside a very tight circle knew that I

was behind the station. People didn't even know where it was being broadcast from. I didn't want anyone linking me to the radio station as I had to do business with the competition. I was only known for my role with Federation.

I would be down in 95FM doing business with them on adverts for Federation and they would say, 'Sure you are advertising with Galaxy.' I would tell them, 'Ah, sure I give them tickets.' I told them that the lads on Galaxy were just giving out a few free tickets live on air to their listeners.

We had Rick O'Shea and Wes D'Arcy from 2FM at a number of the Federation events. They would give respect to Galaxy FM and we would record them and re-broadcast the recordings as ads. 2FM and 95FM rang us, asking what was going on. I just played dumb and said I didn't know, that Galaxy must have recorded it off their website. I said I'd see if I could get a hold of the boys and have a chat with them.

With the radio station broadcasting around the clock, the teen events business was booming. I couldn't believe how busy it got in such a short space of time

We soon discovered the easiest way to prevent problems at a teen event was to keep them interested in what was happening on the stage. We had five of Ireland's best club DJs, massive laser shows, fire walkers, indoor fireworks, give-aways and special guest MCs. We kept things happening. They couldn't take their eyes off the stage or they would miss something. We had them so busy with the entertainment that they didn't have time to get into trouble.

Soon we were attracting crowds of up to 2,000 kids. We held The Ultimate UNICEF Party in association with 2FM, Coca Cola and Galaxy. It was a massive outdoor event in a marquee and we had Wes Darcy from 2FM as master of ceremonies, along with Mark Cage, Darren D and Mossie G. Gerry Ryan sent down Evelyn O'Rourke to report on the event. The plan was that we would be live on air with Gerry the morning after.

The highlight of the show that night was to be an appearance by Special D. He was massive at the time and it was unheard of for an act of that size to appear at a teen event. The night before our event he was performing in Germany. Disaster struck when he missed his flight from Hamburg Airport. His agent called and said that even if he got the next flight from Hamburg, he wouldn't make the gig, and asked if we could put it back twenty-four hours.

Special D lived in Hamburg so I thought he might have just slept in. But at that stage it didn't really matter what the reason was because there was no way he would get to Limerick in time for the gig. At each one of these events things were incredibly tight because of the size of the productions. The tickets might have been expensive, but most of that money was being spent on the acts, the light show and the security. It was shaping up to be a total flop and if we had to refund the tickets, we'd be out of business. We were just hours away from having 1,000 screaming kids on the floor and we needed to do something fast. The last thing we wanted was trouble while a national broadcaster was there. And that would have only been the start of it. Outraged parents would soon be calling *Liveline*, chanting 'Down with that sort of thing' like extras from *Father Ted*. The stress was unbelievable. This was the highest-profile event we had run and it had cost thousands of euro in fees for all the acts, never mind the other expenses.

But I didn't panic. I had phone numbers and contacts, so I called a source in the UK entertainment industry and managed to get hold of 3 of a Kind, who were No. 1 in the UK charts that week. They needed to be on the move within an hour if they were to get to Limerick on time, so I got them lifted from where they were staying and their manager put them on a plane direct to Shannon Airport.

Once 3 of a Kind arrived safely, there was a great feeling of relief. They may have been a one hit wonder, but that week was their moment of fame and we were sure the crowd would love them.

The teenagers were all hyped up waiting for Special D, and Wes Darcy was doing a great job introducing all the local DJs and the UK talent. The place was really getting pumped up and the music was hammering out.

Then Wes told the crowd that there was a problem. He announced that Special D hadn't managed to make his flight to Ireland. The crowd immediately started getting angry and shouting abuse. Wes said, 'But we don't give a fuck,' which stopped them in their tracks. He told them to put their hands together because we had a far bigger and far better act instead. The tension was rising as the crowd waited to hear who was next on stage. He paused briefly, like a reality TV host announcing the winner, before saying, '3 of a Kind!' The band jumped onto the stage and the entire venue erupted. It was like 1,000 teenagers had been plugged into the mains. Special D was forgotten and the night was saved. We brought in an act that was twenty times bigger and they smashed it on stage.

The next morning we took up thirty minutes of airtime on Gerry Ryan's show, talking about the

gig. They interviewed some of the parents about
why they allowed their kids to attend a Federation
event and they also recorded the reaction of the
teens. For us it was a high-risk strategy because
one bad word from Gerry could bring us down. But
we needn't have worried. Gerry gave the biggest
respect to Federation and said it was one of the
most organised teenage events in the country and
that he would let his own daughter go to our events.
It was the best free advertising you could ever hope
to get. We used the audio from the *Gerry Ryan Show*
to promote Federation everywhere we went, and it
went down a storm.

We even thought about setting up a security
company because we were paying so much to an
outside company. We were doing so many gigs
that it made sense for us to do it ourselves. Then
we would be able to provide event management,
entertainment and even security, so we would
became a one-stop shop for running events.

After the *Gerry Ryan Show* we needed to expand
across Munster to capitalise on the publicity. There
was already a rival teen event running in Cork so we
knew there was a market there. All we needed to do
was to convince the Cork teens that the Federation
events were the best.

Before moving into any area it is vital to conduct

a bit of market research to see who the main competitors are and what sort of event they are offering. In Cork there was nothing extraordinary; in fact the entertainment on offer was pretty tame. The plan was simple. We went down to 'the real capital' with a group of promotion staff. I paid a courtesy visit to the local garda sergeant and told him that a group of my staff would be handing out flyers for a new event we were planning, outside Cork City Hall, where our rivals were holding an event that night. The staff were instructed to hand out the flyers to the kids as they left the venue and say: 'See you again next month,' nothing else. It was guerrilla marketing and the rival organiser went completely mad. The gardaí arrived but I went up to the first officer and told him I had spoken with his boss, and he allowed us to continue.

The next stroke was to book the venue one week before our rival. Teenagers might be let out to an event once a month, but it is unlikely they would get out two weekends in a row, so we needed to get in before the competition.

At that stage, tickets were being sold in record stores. It was before internet booking and Ticketmaster were so popular. I noticed a flyer in one shop advertising the rival event and went in and spoke to the boss. He said the rival operator was giving them a commission of €1 per ticket. I offered him €2 a ticket. I handed him 1,000 tickets and then told him about my new 'special bonus scheme'. I explained the scheme to him by pulling out a wad of cash and peeling off €50 notes. When I reached €1,000, I handed over the cash and said he could keep the money if he sold the 1,000 tickets. If he only sold 999, then he'd have to give back the money. He'd could still have up to €1,998 in commission but he'd lose the bonus.

So you can imagine what happened when a kid went in looking for a ticket. The guys in the shop played their part very well. They told the kids that the Federation event was the best night out and very few tickets were sold for the other gig. The competition didn't know what hit them.

We got the gigs up and running in Cork but we were under serious pressure. Our rivals upped their game and invested in better quality acts. It was time to bring out the big guns. There was only one way to beat them, and that was to launch Galaxy FM in Cork.

FM radio works by line of sight – if you can see it, you can broadcast to it. So there was no way a signal could get from Limerick to Cork. We needed to locate a transmitter somewhere in the city. My tech guy came to Cork with me to see if there was anywhere we could set up a transmitter. The main pirate station in Cork was Kiss FM and they were running a very high-powered, tight signal. We drove around for an hour following their signal with a hand-held scanning device that could tell you where a broadcast was coming from. We tracked the signal down to a building in Knocknaheany, on the outskirts of Cork City. The tech guy nodded and pointed towards the aerial.

We approached a guy who was working outside the building and asked him about the transmitter. He nearly had a heart attack, thinking we were the BCI and were coming to arrest him. He said the transmitter and aerial weren't his and that the guys from the radio station had promised him cash if he allowed them to use his property. Then he said he hadn't been paid yet, and I spotted an opening.

We came to an agreement that he would rent us the location for the aerial. He would seize Kiss FM's equipment until they paid him the money they owed. I handed him the €1,000 that he claimed was due to him from Kiss FM and I promised more cash in the future. I simply asked him not to interfere with the equipment and to keep it until the Kiss FM people had paid him the back rent. My tech guy retuned their transmitter to kill their signal in preparation for the Cork launch of Galaxy FM.

The brilliant aspect of this approach was that Kiss FM couldn't go to the authorities and ask for their illegal broadcast equipment back.

To start off we ran pre-recorded shows in Cork, but later we linked live from Limerick. Before the live links started we needed a way of bringing the shows to Cork over the internet. We couldn't get broadband for almost a month, so instead we approached a friend and gave her a computer. This girl was doing some promotions work for us in Cork. She lived with her mother, just across from our new transmitter. She said we could put up an aerial at the rear of her house so we could link in with the new transmitter. We sent the signal over the internet from the girl's new computer through the aerial and into our new transmitter, which blasted it across the city. We told the girl's mother, quite shamelessly, that we were from Sky TV and we were installing a better aerial so she could get extra channels. Little did she know that the new aerial was a vital cog in our plan to crack Cork City.

The next stage was to flood the city with car stickers promoting Galaxy FM. We had promotions girls standing on all the busy junctions in branded T-shirts, handing out the stickers. It was very slick. Soon we were taking live phone calls on air from Cork and we built up a listenership very quickly.

The buzz was unbelievable. The gigs in Cork and Limerick were both doing well and bringing in revenue. Tipperary came on stream after that. Then we started in Galway and Waterford. We even went up to Enniskillen. Nothing could stop our advance across the country.

Selling the tickets was only one way of making money and the ticket sales alone wouldn't necessarily put you in profit. On some of these events, the tickets would only cover the cost of the artists, security and venue hire. Once, we had eleven acts from the UK at an event lasting five hours, with ten DJs and 1,000 teenagers. It costs a lot to stage that kind of event. Sometimes, despite having a full house, the only profit would come from the mineral bar and the cloakroom. I was always on the hunt for new ways to increase revenue.

At one event in Cork we slipped up and we didn't have any hot food arranged. That was a significant blunder. Hot dogs and burgers were a massive earner. Normally we had special hot dog machines that could heat hundreds of them in an hour. They would then be packed in special warmer bags and sold around the venue. But this weekend we had nothing arranged and it could have made the difference between turning a profit and making a loss on the night.

That morning as I was driving into Cork, I saw a sign for McDonald's advertising their Eurosaver Menu. They were selling burgers for €1 each. Immediately I started working out if there was any way of turning the idea in my head into a profit. The kids would easily spend €3 on a burger, especially when there was nothing else available. I walked into the restaurant, went up to the counter and told the guy I wanted 1,000 burgers. He was completely dumbfounded. He just looked at me and then over at one of his colleagues, who came over to talk to me. They couldn't imagine why someone would order 1,000 burgers. I think they thought there was a hidden camera somewhere and they were being filmed for TV.

Eventually a manager came out and I told him I was entirely serious and took out a roll of €50 notes. I peeled off twenty of them and told him again that I wanted 1,000 burgers. Once he saw the cash, there wasn't a problem. I went out to the van and brought in the food warmers, which would keep the burgers warm for hours. They stacked all the burgers in the bags for me and that was that – sorted!

I didn't mind the customers seeing the McDonald's wrapper on the burgers. It made it look like we were an even bigger production. The staff strapped on the bags and went hawking the burgers through the gig. I spent €1,000 on burgers. All I had to do was shift 333 of them to break even. I could have had all those burgers going home with me if they didn't sell. But luckily they were a great hit and we could have shifted twice as many.

We had to constantly improve and develop the events. The size of the production was increasing and so were the risks. We brought in rappers, dancers, fire-eaters and snake handlers. Our tickets were now being sold by Ticketmaster, which added extra credibility and made the events seem more grown up. All our promotion emphasised the scale of the events and that tickets were selling out quickly, which created a buzz.

Some weeks we might try a new venue, and it wasn't always a success. If not enough tickets sold then the atmosphere would be dead, and after everyone was paid there could be a substantial loss. But that was all part of trying to grow a business. You have to experiment. Whether something goes well or badly, you can learn from the experience and improve your product.

In the end the competition in Cork got so hot that we had to keep raising the bar. I was spending more and more time down there, and we were putting so much money into the events that it became difficult to turn a profit. A big Radio 1 DJ from the UK could charge €7,000 just to accept the booking. I became disillusioned with it and one day I just said, 'I'm not fighting like this anymore. It's not worth the hassle.' I made the decision to stop running events in Cork and to turn off the Galaxy transmitter there.

The problem was that Federation and Galaxy had taken up so much of my time that I couldn't keep the original DJ business in Limerick going. Looking back now, I probably got too big too quickly. I should have stayed with Galaxy and used it to promote just one or two gigs. Steve Collins said to me one day, 'Look after the small work and the big work will look after itself.' That's what I failed to do. The Limerick DJ scene had been too much trouble for me to continue while I was chasing the big prize. I was so busy with running events and taking on event management work from major companies that I had let the little stuff go.

Two years earlier I was happy running my ten DJs, taking €50 a night from all of them as well as the €200 for my own gig. That's €700 for a night's work, but I was too focused on breaking the next level to be happy with it.

I was proud of what I had done in the teen market, and I knew the experience would stand to me, but it was time to move on. So when I got the opportunity to run my own nightclub, I jumped at it. It wasn't the wisest decision I have ever made.

THREE

CLUBBED TO DEATH

I am a very driven person. Anyone who gets to know me will figure that out in a few minutes. I'm always on the hunt for the next big thing. Most days I'm up before 8 a.m. and it's the early hours of the morning before I get home. You'll never make any money sitting on the couch in your living room, watching daytime TV.

Federation and Galaxy were flying in the summer of 2007. I had got to know a man called Joe Clarke very well through running some of our events at his club. Joe was a very well-known and respected figure on the Limerick nightclub scene. He and Pat Barry ran the Trinity Rooms, in Limerick City Centre. The club was the top nightspot in the city and was among the best clubs in the entire country.

The Trinity Rooms attracted the best acts and Joe always knew exactly what the punters wanted. Joe had been a great help to me with Federation, putting me in touch with many of the promoters, agents and acts that we used.

The Trinity Rooms opened around 2003 in the old Granary Building on Michael Street. It was an ideal location for a club as it was in the city centre, overlooking the River Shannon. It had won numerous industry awards and was a very well-designed club. It was divided into three distinct areas and there were a couple of courtyard areas, which worked exceptionally well because people could take time out from dancing and just chill out. No expense was spared on the fit-out and at the time there was nothing else like it in the city. It was very professionally run and, importantly, no troublemakers were allowed in.

The Trinity Rooms secured the likes of Moloko, Ash and The Fun Lovin' Criminals. While Joe was behind the club, it was constantly in the media because of the high quality of its entertainment. Negative stories were very rare and that was an achievement, considering what is normally written about the city.

In September 2007 Joe approached me with a business proposition. I was very flattered when he came to me because the Trinity Rooms was a genuine success story. He told me that Coolio's nightclub in Newcastle West was available for lease and that the terms were pretty good. He felt it was a great opportunity to expand the Trinity Rooms and for me it was a chance to become involved with one of the top clubs in Ireland.

Joe explained that Coolio's was available on a three-year lease. The landlord was looking for a short-term deal as the building was earmarked for redevelopment as a bistro, bar and nightclub. The landlord was planning to create a landmark development. That part of Newcastle West was going to be completely regenerated and the best part was that whoever took the short-term lease would also have first option on the rebuilt premises.

Joe had worked in Coolio's before and he knew the area very well. Newcastle West is a medieval market town approximately twenty minutes' drive from Limerick City. It is on the main road to Killarney and the South West. It has a massive hinterland area, which meant it could draw in customers from far and wide. A top-quality club could attract punters from as far away as Castleisland in County Kerry and even Charleville and Kanturk in County Cork.

I had worked with Coolio's in the past, running a night called Temptation. It was mostly 80s and 90s music with a few recent chart hits thrown in. I sent down my best DJ, Mr Alan, to cover the night. Alan O'Donnell knew exactly how to run a party night and keep the crowd hopping. We ran Temptation for a good few months and it showed that the venue had plenty of potential and that the people of Newcastle West enjoyed a good night out.

The decision to open the club was very rushed. Joe shook hands with the landlord and agreed the deal. We started construction within forty-eight hours of the initial approach. That's how convinced we were that the club was going to be a major success.

The plan was fairly simple. It was obvious that money would have to be spent on refurbishing the building, even though it was going to be knocked down three years later. But the Trinity Rooms was an award-winning nightclub and had won plaudits for its design and layout, so there was no need to reinvent the wheel, as we already had the ideal template. Effectively, the plan was to cut and paste the Trinity Rooms design and brand the new club, called West. The paint scheme, logos and lighting rigs would all be the same. The Newcastle West building was smaller and it didn't have the same character, but with careful planning we could create the right atmosphere.

The business plan was also fairly simple. Joe Clarke and Pat Barry had set up a company called Seafront Entertainment for a Dublin-based venture that never happened. It was decided that Seafront Entertainment could be used as the company behind the new club. The shares would be split equally three ways, and each partner would invest €100,000. The company's shareholding was limited to ninety shares and each of us would receive thirty.

We agreed that I would take care of the construction and Joe would deal with the suppliers, arranging meetings and getting quotations for equipment. Pat was a silent partner and didn't play an active role in the club. I had been doing some consultancy work for nightclubs around Munster, advising them on entertainment and how to organise high-profile nights, so this was a golden opportunity to use my knowledge in my own club.

Between us, we had plenty of experience and we knew the venue and the town, so in the end there wasn't that much to consider. I was always willing to take a gamble, but this was like backing Brazil to beat a team of pensioners. You could take it to the bank.

The landlord agreed €60,000 rent in advance for the first year because the club needed to be completely refurbished. Because the building was

in such a poor state, our refurbishment work would
be in lieu of the security deposit. Joe and I stood in
the middle of the club one day and we could see how
it was going to work; we were able to imagine the
place full of paying punters and we knew exactly
which walls we wanted to pull down and what we
wanted to put where. But the building was very old-
fashioned and everything had to be ripped out and
replaced. It would need a huge amount of work to
bring it up to a high enough standard and we agreed
that there would need to be some reconstruction to
give the club the wow factor.

The budget to open the club was about
€300,000. We were hoping that my experience
in the construction industry would help to keep
reconstruction costs down. I was well used to
working on building sites and I could project manage
everything and hopefully speed up the work.

We got the keys in October 2007 and work
started almost immediately. We had a very tight
deadline because we wanted the club to be open for
Christmas. The plan was to have Katy French and a
fashion show with a string of top models from the
Assets agency on the launch night.

The building became a hive of activity and I
was almost like a prisoner on the site. I was the
project manager, foreman and builder. There were

tradesmen everywhere, people with measuring tapes, talking on mobile phones and organising things. Joe was making all the phone calls from the office, arranging things like advertising, public relations, branding and equipment for the nightclub. He was also dealing with the accountants and the legal side of things.

Working on an old building will always present unforeseen problems. Unexpected structural issues can turn a simple half-hour job into a week-long major operation. Every time we hit a problem, it ate into the investment capital and pushed back the opening night. We needed the club to open as soon as possible so the money tap could be turned on and we could get the cash flow going.

The biggest problem we ran into was the water supply. We couldn't get enough water into the building with the existing supply. To meet our needs we would have to tap into the water main. But to find it we had to dig up half of the car park. It was a disaster. This was completely unforeseen and it cost so much time and money that it threatened to halt the project.

In late October or early November 2007 Mike Bridgeman called me. He owned a sex shop in Limerick, near where my father had his market stall, and was interested in getting into the entertainment business. He and I had looked at a couple of nightclubs and bars in the past but nothing ever came of it. I was involved in event management and had looked at a lot of potential business opportunities across the sector with a lot of different people. Bridgeman also had a video production company and he had done some work for me in the past. He had some impressive video cameras, like ones you would see on film sets.

Mike said he had heard that I was opening a nightclub in Newcastle West. I told him that I was only looking after the construction work and that the club was going to be run by Joe Clarke and Pat Barry from the Trinity Rooms. I let on that I was just the builder because I thought the link to the Trinity Rooms in Limerick would create far more hype. Also, I didn't want to let Bridgeman know that I was involved in the venture because we had looked at a number of clubs together earlier. We were never business partners and we never had any formal arrangement, but I didn't want an awkward conversation with him either. Joe had approached me directly with this project because of how well we had worked together previously. When I went to see venues with Bridgeman in the past I was there as an advisor or a consultant. I often advised club owners about how to improve their entertainment and get some customers through the door. Bridgeman wanted my advice on whether projects were viable. We saw one club in Kilmallock, County Limerick that was available for lease, but there were a number of significant problems with the venue, so I advised Bridgeman against getting involved. He was raring to go but I could see pitfalls that would have cost a lot of money. Joe and I had a good team between ourselves, so another investor at that stage was not necessary.

Bridgeman told me: 'That was always my idea, to open that place.' I didn't think too much about the conversation at the time, as I was too busy trying to get things completed.

It was fairly clear by the middle of November that the Christmas deadline wasn't realistic. There was still too much construction work to be done and there were funding issues. By that stage I had paid out between €80,000 and €90,000 for materials and contractors' fees.

Around Christmas 2007 Joe and I had a meeting in the Maldron Hotel. A significant amount of money and time had already been invested and I told Joe that I was approaching my limit and I couldn't keep putting cash into the club with no return. I needed Joe and Pat to release funds because the pressure was on to get the club opened. The poor state of the building had delayed the refurbishment, which had already pushed back the opening date to 15 February 2008. I showed him a folder of all my invoices and he sat there, scratching his head.

'There isn't that much spent already, is there?' he asked.

He told me that he wasn't really in a position to increase the amount he was putting into the club because of issues at the Trinity Rooms.

Joe said: 'I don't really have the money to go any further because I was promised a loan off Pat and he can't give me that loan now because he doesn't have the money himself to put in for his shares.'

I said, 'Joe, I'm after putting a lot of money into this and I can't go any further.'

Joe told me that the Trinity Rooms was having issues with the fire officer and the landlord. He said that Pat had used the money earmarked for our club in one of his other business ventures that needed a cash boost. He said if I could make up the difference he would be happy to stay involved in the club.

We both knew that the club was going to make money and it wasn't too far from completion. It was too late to stop the project as we had already invested so much. That money would have been lost if we pulled the plug. We just did not have enough money to finish the job to a high-quality standard. In late

2007 and early 2008 credit was rapidly drying up. The recession had not yet hit but the storm clouds were definitely on the horizon. Months earlier the banks were handing out cash like it was a limitless resource. Now securing finance had turned into a search for the Holy Grail.

I knew one guy who might have wanted to get involved in the club. He was a good pal and we had done a lot of business in the past. He said he was very interested but Christmas wasn't a great time for him to look at a new business as he was flat out. If it was a few months earlier or later he wouldn't have had a problem investing. Unfortunately, the February deadline had now become critical and we couldn't wait around. We had started advertising and recruiting staff, and we were running an expensive radio campaign to build up hype. The club had to open so we could start seeing a return on our investment.

It was then that Mike Bridgeman's name came into the conversation. Joe said that Bridgeman had the cash and that he was interested in becoming involved in the project.

We arranged a meeting in the Trinity Rooms to show Bridgeman a template of what the club in Newcastle West would look like. We highlighted the various features from the club that would be copied over to the new venue. The following morning Bridgeman drove out to Newcastle West to inspect the building. He looked around and he was very impressed with the amount of money that had been spent and with the way the place was shaping up. He seemed to be really excited by the prospect of getting on board.

Shortly after that we met again at Bridgeman's house, in Ballyneety. He had a lovely bungalow with a massive pond out the back. It looked quite impressive. His wife was in the kitchen baking bread or scones and the smell was fantastic. This time the club's bookkeeper came to the meeting with me and went through the accounts. After chatting for a while, we got down to business. I showed Bridgeman my folder of invoices and told them that was my expenditure to date. Joe and Pat had decided that they were happy to walk away from the project without any return on their investment. Bridgeman requested that Pat and Joe sign a letter stating that they would no longer have anything to gain from the business or have any interest in the company. So if Bridgeman came on board we would be the two shareholders. I showed him exactly how much money we had spent and how much was needed to complete the project.

I asked Bridgeman if he was prepared to invest

and take Joe and Pat's positions in the company. He said he was very interested. He spent around ten minutes looking through the invoices and said, 'I am very impressed. For the amount of work that's done for this price, I am very impressed.' He said that if we had brought in a contract builder, the bill would have been three times higher.

He walked out to the kitchen and I was hoping he was going to bring in one of his wife's scones. Instead he returned with a cheque for €20,000 and handed it over to the bookkeeper. He told the bookkeeper to lodge the money into the company account that was about to be set up. Bridgeman signed the bank account documentation as a signatory of the new account and as a director of the company. He would become a director as soon as he signed the legal papers and returned them to the company solictor. He said, 'I'm in.' I hadn't expected to get a cheque that evening but it was a huge relief and it was enough to get things moving again and hopefully to get the club opened.

The extra cash bought us some time but it was still a struggle to meet the 15 February deadline.

We had been running extensive advertising on Spin South West FM, first looking for staff and then advertising the opening. That money would have been wasted if we didn't make our deadline. Also, once the publicity had started, failure to open on time could have been fatal to the future success of the operation.

From October to December I was on site seven days a week, from 7 a.m. until 9 or 10 o'clock at night. I spent all of January and February down there. I didn't see my family at all. I wasn't thinking of anything else. All the gigs stopped and I shut everything down to concentrate on the club. I gave everything up for that club. Bridgeman spent as many hours on site as I did. He put 100 per cent in, too. He was genuinely excited about what he was getting involved in.

We actually lived on site for two weeks before the club opened, with shifts going on around the clock. Construction workers would leave in the evening and then the painters would come in and work by floodlight through the night. Mike and I lived in his camper van outside the club. We were getting along great and we were both very focused on getting the job done.

We employed a guy called Mike Shaughnessy to manage the club. He had lots of experience and was a Newcastle West local, which meant he knew the clientele and, more importantly, who the troublemakers were. He and his wife came on board and he took on the bar staff and would look after the day-to-day running of the club when it opened.

We had an excellent security system in place that used high-resolution CCTV cameras. As soon as someone approached the club they would be on camera. In the back office we had a local guy who knew every unsavoury character in the town. He would be able to see everything on the CCTV but nobody would be able to see him, so he couldn't be intimidated. All the security staff had earpieces and microphones, so when the guy in the back office spotted an anti-social character, he could be pulled aside and told he wasn't getting in. Most of the security staff were Polish, Russian or Lithuanian and had no connection with Newcastle West. The rougher types couldn't understand how these foreign lads knew who they were and that they had a history of causing trouble.

During Valentine's week there was still an enormous amount of work to complete. Valentine's night was the Thursday and the big invite-only opening night was slated for the Friday. Saturday was the first night with customers paying on the door. We wanted to have a soft opening – a trial night – before the actual launch. It was Rag Week at the University of Limerick, so we organised a mystery tour for the students. We were going to bring 1,000 of them the twenty odd miles to Newcastle West and let them have a night in the club.

The student night would be a great chance to test out all of the club's systems in advance of the first 'real' customers. Even with the best plans there will always be problems. The soft opening was a chance to expose these problems so the real night would go off without a hitch. The security, bar, lighting, music – everything would be tested that night and we'd learn all the hiccups.

We were ready to go when the fire officer called a halt to everything. He wanted the best possible fire system in place, to offer the highest level of protection. He said we didn't have enough sensors and, without his blessing, the club couldn't open. There was no point crying or complaining because the man had made his ruling and we just had to accept it and put things right. If he had asked me to strip naked, shave off my hair and run through the middle of town singing 'The Fields of Athenry', I'd have done it in a heartbeat.

The soft opening was cancelled and now the students' mystery tour was a mystery even to us. We had a matter of hours to find somewhere for 1,000 thirsty students. I rang a pal who had a club in Ennis and told him about my problem and asked if he would be able to cater for the group. I think he thought all his birthdays had come at once, so at least we had sorted out the problem of the students.

The company that was looking after the fire alarm system couldn't get it working the way the fire officer wanted, so we had to get a new company in. They worked through the night and the next day to get it up to spec.

Missing the pre-opening night was a misfortune. It would have been nice to open with a few thousand euro in the till. But missing the official opening would have been a disaster and the club would probably never have recovered because we had hyped up the opening so much. We had even started a rumour that we were building a five-million-euro celebrity super club.

Bridgeman was suffering with stress at this stage. We had been working extremely hard over the previous month and nobody had been getting much sleep. The failure to get the fire cert had ratcheted up the pressure. Bridgeman was very testy on opening day, when the fire officer returned. He was nipping at anyone he came across and you could see he was very anxious about the launch. I was talking to the fire officer when Bridgeman came over, shouting. He asked me if I had allowed the nightclub manager to buy a suit so he could look like the bouncers. At the time I didn't care whether he had bought a suit or not – I had more important things on my mind.

Bridgeman persisted, 'Did you give that authorisation?'

I told him if the manager wanted to get a suit, he could get a fucking suit.

'But you shouldn't have done that without consulting us,' he said.

We had given the okay for fifteen security staff to get suits. The manager needed a suit, as he was the one who would be meeting and greeting the customers and VIPs. He was the face of the club and he needed to look the part.

'Mike, just relax. We'll deal with the suit in a minute,' I told him.

The fire officer got back to business and checked the rest of the building. We got the clearance an hour before we opened. That was far too tight for my liking, but at least we could open the club and start recouping our investment. The opening Friday night was by invitation only. This created a bit of buzz around the town, but in reality it wasn't that hard to get your hands on a ticket. All you had to do was send us an email. But if you hadn't planned in advance you weren't getting in.

We also sent invites to all the local businesses and factories. We wanted a particular type of clientele. We didn't go out on the streets to hand out invites because we wanted to set a standard and build up the club's reputation. If we let in a crowd of gougers, we'd never recover from that.

I surveyed the club before we opened and I couldn't help but be proud of what we had achieved. Everything was ready; everything was spot on. The club looked incredibly modern and we had the best quality lighting systems, lasers, massive plasma screens – the works. Nothing like this had ever been seen in rural Ireland. It was going to blow the socks off every other club in the area. Now we just had to make money!

It was a matter of minutes until the doors were opened for the first time. We had a few final briefings with the staff and had the security guys prepared. I looked out the door and the crowd was massive. People were standing there with their invitations in their hands, dying to see Newcastle West's new super club. Everyone was dressed up and it was exactly the type of clientele we were looking for.

The entire evening was being broadcast live on SPIN South West FM. It was their first ever live outside broadcast. The club was packed to capacity that night. Everyone was having a good time. It was free entry but we could have filled the club again with paying customers. There were probably 1,500 people in the queue outside looking to come in. We had to tell them there was no room and that the club would be open at 10 p.m. the following night. There was huge relief that everything had worked so well for the launch, but we still had to pull off a full-price night.

On Saturday the club was packed to the rafters again – this time with paying customers. We were charging €12 on the door and it was €2 to check your coat. Everyone in the club would have two or three drinks each, which was at least a further €10. The night went like clockwork again and it seemed that all the hard work and sacrifice were paying off.

When the last of the punters had left, we sat in the VIP area and chilled out for a while. We'd probably have to come in on Monday morning to let in the cleaners and bottle up. We'd have a meeting then to see where we could make improvements and to plan the promotional work to make sure the club was packed the next weekend. But 4 a.m. after a successful night was not the time to be worrying about that. All I wanted to do was get home and climb in my own bed and sleep. Sunday was going to be a day for the family and relaxation.

As we were about to leave, Mike Shaughnessy, the manager, came out of the cash room with the weekend's takings in a large moneybag. I didn't want to handle the cash, as I didn't have a safe. Anytime I had run a club night and money was being collected on the door, I never took part in collecting it. I'd let the club take the money and I'd collect the ticket stub. That way we'd know how many tickets had been sold and how much cash we were due. It was simple and it meant that no one could be ripped off.

Bridgeman volunteered to take the money home and put it in his safe. Mike Shaughnessy had put a detailed note in the cash bag, with the amount of money and the number of the individual notes. The turnover for the weekend was in the region of €43,000. We were jubilant when we heard this. It was our first cash night and we were making money. The pressure evaporated because it was clear the club was going to be a success. All that was left to be done was turn off the lights, lock the door and go home. We all said our goodbyes and I sat into my jeep and drove home to Limerick.

I wanted to spend Sunday with my family so I could reintroduce myself to my son Lee. It was so long since he had seen me he might not have remembered what I look like. Seeing all those people on the dance floor and the queues of people trying to get into the club proved that the hard work had been worth it. Now it was going to be payback time for my family.

I could get back to being a proper father again.

I was relaxing at home on Sunday morning with my family around me. I was still very tired but I was relieved too. I was in great humour until the phone rang. It had emerged there was €15,000 missing from the takings. There had also been a major row in the centre of Newcastle West between the manager, Mike Shaughnessy, and Mike Bridgeman. Shaughnessy had counted the total amount of cash as well as the total number of individual notes and filled out a form detailing the exact amount of cash taken over the weekend. When he took the cash home, Bridgeman re-counted the money and he believed there was €15,000 missing. He immediately went to Newcastle West to confront Mike Shaughnessy.

Bridgeman found Shaughnessy in the middle of the town and accused him there and then of stealing the cash. According to Shaughnessy, Bridgeman then assaulted him.

My plans for a day off were scuppered and I had to return to Newcastle West. It was my first day off in almost five months and I had to deal with this. If there was money missing from the bag it should have waited until Monday, when we could have called in Mike Shaughnessy for a meeting, instead of accusing him of theft in front of half of Newcastle West.

Mike Shaughnessy called the gardaí and made

a complaint about Bridgeman. He also instructed his solicitor to sue Bridgeman, Joe Clarke and me for libel and constructive dismissal. Joe and I were included because we were directors of the company, although neither of us had any involvement in the incident.

I'm certain that Mike Shaughnessy did not take a penny. He did a great job that opening weekend and was as committed to making the club a success as any of us. In any case, no one would be stupid enough to count a weekend's takings, write down the amount and then steal €15,000 from the total you had just accounted for.

This was week one and Mike Shaughnessy was the only person with the details of the staff roster and who was to get paid how much. No one else had this information and Mike was working from his office at home. Now we were faced with a situation where the staff were due in the following Friday, expecting to get paid, and we didn't have a clue who was owed what.

After such a successful opening, we now had a major disaster on our hands. We had lost our manager and we were alienating our customers by accusing a well-respected member of their community of stealing.

I was willing to write off the fifteen grand and

put it down to a learning experience. I knew we could make it back soon enough if the club was running properly. I met with Mike Shaughnessy's solicitor and went through what he had belonging to the club. We asked for all club property to be returned through his solicitor and I signed for everything.

Mike was in the meeting and as it was about to finish he said, 'If I wanted to steal money, I could have, and you wouldn't even know.'

'How could you have done that?' I asked.

'The till company showed me how to set everything up; they didn't show you. I don't even think you know how to use them.'

He outlined in detail how someone could defraud the company without detection. He said he could have run the tills in such a way that he could cancel all the transactions over a one-hour period and pocket the cash. He knew the system so well that if he wanted to steal €15,000 he could have easily done it without ever being caught. He could have gotten away with €100,000 within the space of a few months, given his notice and left, and we would never know. I went away and checked it out and it all made sense. There was just no way that he would have taken the money.

On the opening night and the second night, all

the locals were approaching Mike Shaughnessy and congratulating him on the fantastic new club. I don't think Bridgeman liked that. He wasn't getting the credit he thought was due to him. I wasn't interested in people patting me on the back or telling me I was a great man. I was down there for one reason – to make money. If I was going down there for people to tell me I was a great chap, I should have stayed at home.

By Tuesday we had the gardaí on to us about assault complaints. They said that a complaint had been made and they were investigating what had happened. They did not arrest anyone and nobody was charged. Bridgeman told the guards that he was the owner of the place and that he was the licensee. For a company to operate it needs at least two directors and only a director can be a licensee. Bridgeman had not yet signed the documentation to make him a director, so Joe Clarke had remained a director and the licence was in his name, despite the fact that he was no longer involved in the business.

We had all agreed that the licence would stay under Joe's name because we couldn't miss the 15 February deadline. But Mike didn't have the common sense when he was talking to the guards to say that either he or I were going to take over as licensee from Joe Clarke when Bridgeman replaced him as a director.

The gardaí had all the correct information and if you tell them something different they immediately become suspicious. They suddenly think you are trying to hide something or that there is something untoward going on. The last thing we needed was the gardaí breathing down our necks.

Our claims in the promotional material about a five-million-euro super club were about to come back and bite us, as the Criminal Assets Bureau (CAB) had been reading the newspapers. Tales of large amounts of cash disappearing whetted their appetite, and soon we were on their radar.

❖ ❖ ❖

FOUR

HARD KNOCK LIFE

It was like something out of a Greek tragedy – or a poorly acted television drama. West was facing disaster after operating for just one weekend. Our manager was gone and when the staff heard exactly what had happened, they were not happy. Many of them had been friendly with Mike Shaughnessy and he was very well respected in Newcastle West. The locals didn't believe that Mike had been involved in any type of theft and it clearly showed the following weekend.

When we opened the doors on the next Friday, there were no long queues of eager revellers. The previous week everyone had been saying that West was the best club in the county; now it was the place run by 'those Limerick scumbags'. We may have been from the same county and we all followed Munster in the rugby and Limerick in the GAA, but Newcastle West and Limerick City can be worlds apart. It had become 'them and us' and it was a very uncomfortable position to be in.

I was running the club that weekend, with plenty of help from Mike Bridgeman. His assistance was not particularly welcome, as it was hardly good PR, but it was an unfortunate necessity.

Almost 50 per cent of our customers had vanished within a week and the reason was obvious. The entire local market had been alienated because one of their own had been wrongly accused. This had turned into our very own iceberg moment. We may have been holed below the waterline but I was determined that West was not going down.

Joe Clarke was soon on the phone and he was very agitated. He had just received the solicitor's letter from Mike Shaughnessy's legal team because he was still named as a director and as licensee on the company documents. The plan had been to transfer the licence to either Bridgeman or me once the club was up and running, as this would be quicker and less hassle than making an application for a new one. But now that there were doubts over the future of the club, Bridgeman was becoming reluctant.

It was as if a self-destruct button had been

pressed. Up until the club opened we had been working very well together. Bridgeman was anxious to make the club a success and for the few weeks between Christmas and the opening night, he was on site as much as everyone else. There was no doubting his commitment. But now he was acting very erratically and he was starting to get worried about the falling numbers. It was becoming increasingly difficult to work with him. He had a quick temper and was not well liked by the staff. In my experience, working with people in a calm manner produces better results than shouting. But I was conscious that Bridgeman was my business partner and I needed him on board to make the club a success.

At the time of the opening we had approximately €250,000 worth of stock on the premises, all of it on credit. It was enough drink to last us about three or four weeks. We had a month to pay for it, which wouldn't be a problem as long as we had enough customers coming through the door. But the bottom line was that if we didn't sell enough drink, we couldn't pay for the stock we were holding.

The club had a very clever stock control system to reduce theft. There were electronic counters on the bottle openers, spirit optic units and on the beer pumps. No matter what was served or opened, it went into the computer. With such a large amount of stock it would be easy for some of it to 'wander off'. But a rigorous stock control system prevented people from handing out free drinks to their mates, because it all had to be accounted for.

After the second week, it was clear that the missing €15,000 was the least of our worries. The take was well down on the previous week and it was clear that many of Mike Shaughnessy's friends were boycotting the club.

I had never intended to become involved in the day-to-day running of the club; I wanted to arrange the spectaculars and special events. But now I was spending my time trying to ensure that the staff got paid and that the supplies were replenished. I had to arrange everything from toilet cleaner to bottles of Jägermeister.

Bridgeman had his own plan to make up the losses. We had been running a very tight entrance policy, preventing known troublemakers from getting in. The gardaí had given us some advice about who to watch out for and, with our insider knowledge, we were keeping the place very safe. Bridgeman wanted as many paying customers in the club as possible and was not interested in having a strict door policy. He didn't like the Polish head of security either. In my experience a good door policy is the most effective way of creating a successful club. If people do not feel safe, then they will not want to come in. We wanted customers who were after a good night out, not those who were looking to get loaded with as much alcohol as possible and cause trouble.

Bridgeman said if there was a problem, then the security could throw the troublemakers out. I was against this plan because it ran contrary to everything I had learned in the entertainment business. We had a duty of care to everyone in the club, including the staff. Bridgeman wanted anyone who showed up who wasn't drunk and had the cash to pay on the door to be let in. This immediately changed the atmosphere, as many of the people in the club had been barred from every other place in Newcastle West. Immediately the bouncers were far busier dealing with incidents that threatened the safety of customers. This wasn't how I wanted to go about saving the club's reputation. Bridgeman also insisted that we take on some new security staff of his choosing to work in the venue.

The problems over the ownership of the club were also beginning to surface. The uncertainty around Bridgeman's position created confusion about who was responsible for what. As the weeks passed, the relationship between the club and Bridgeman was deteriorating. He refused to sign cheques to pay creditors and this was becoming a problem. He wanted to be repaid before the creditors got their money.

There was a continuing issue with cash going missing from the club. Each week we would be short somewhere between a few hundred euro and a couple of grand. It was never as much as €15,000 but it was still enough to be noticed and it was all adding up. I made a few discreet attempts to discover how the cash was going missing but I couldn't call in the gardaí after the events of the first week. We had cameras covering the tills to see if it was members of staff, but we couldn't accuse anyone without proper evidence or we would end up with another legal case. Ultimately we had to introduce new cash handling measures, which eliminated any theft. The person behind the missing cash was never found but at least they were unable to 'liberate' any more funds.

Within weeks things had got to a critical stage. A meeting of the shareholders and directors was called and held in the company auditor's office, but Bridgeman failed to show. We discussed the problems that had been affecting the club. The company's solicitor sent Bridgeman a letter ordering him not to have any further involvement with the day-to-day running of the club because, while he was an investor, he was not a director of the business. He was also sent a B10 form that would have made him a director. All he had to do was sign the form. He refused to do this and said that he didn't want to be a director of a sinking ship.

Bridgeman arrived at the club with a couple of Transit vans one afternoon when I wasn't there. He owned one of the laser lights and he had left his Crombie coat behind him one evening. He wanted to remove them from the premises. What he didn't know was that we had security on site during the day on the advice of the company's solicitor. There was a lot of valuable stock in the cellar as well as very expensive audio-visual equipment, and I didn't want any of the company assets to go missing. The security staff restrained him and the gardaí were called. Bridgeman said he wanted to remove some 'personal effects'. The security guys rang me and I told the gardaí that he could take the equipment that he owned.

With Bridgeman out of the picture I immediately reinstated the strict door policy and the undesirable elements were told they were no longer welcome. I also called to Mike Shaughnessy's home to apologise. We sat down in his front room and drank tea. I said I was certain that he had nothing to do with the missing €15,000. I was determined to get him back on board because firstly he was superb at his job, and secondly it would stop the rumours circulating about the club. I was also doing Bridgeman a massive favour by asking Mike Shaughnessy to return. When he came back to work, he withdrew his complaint against Bridgeman and also dropped the wrongful dismissal and defamation cases against the club.

Removing Mike Bridgeman from the day-to-day running of the club immediately lifted the working atmosphere of place. Bridgeman antagonised the staff and shouted at them for no apparent reason. I felt he was out of his depth and could not cope with the pressure. With him gone and Mike Shaughnessy back as manager, I felt things were beginning to look up for West.

That was until Bridgeman started leading bizarre protests outside the club. He was calling for the club to be closed on the grounds that we had a discriminatory door policy. It was like something out of *Father Ted*. One evening he dropped his pants and mooned gardaí who were monitoring the protest. He was doing his best to make it impossible for the club to operate.

Solicitors' letters were flying back and forth between the two parties. Bridgeman was told again that if he signed the B10 form and became a director he could get back on board. Instead he continued his campaign to have the club closed down. I could not understand why he wanted the club to fail when he had invested his own money in the business. He was like a jealous ex-lover saying 'If I can't have her, nobody can.'

The club had the potential to turn a profit of about €1 million a year. All it needed was a bit of time to develop and build up its reputation. As soon as Mike Shaughnessy was back, the locals started returning and the boycott was ended. It was still within our grasp to make West a success. Bridgeman still could have come back and made a fortune. It might have proved difficult for him to have a role in the day-to-day running of the business, but he could have still benefited from its success.

The club was buzzing again and the queues outside the door had returned. The tills were ringing and we were trying new ways of increasing our profits. One of the most successful ideas was the foam parties, at which we used huge foam guns to cover the dance floors in suds. The club also began opening on Sunday afternoons, giving local bands and DJs a chance to perform and gain experience. Then on Sunday evenings we held an 80s and 90s night for a slightly older audience.

This was a crowd who would not have been in the club on a Friday or a Saturday night and it was a great way to expand our market.

Drawing on my experience with the teenage events, we started to serve food. We used the beer garden as a barbeque area, serving burgers, hot dogs and other hot food. Friday night was Ladies' Night. Women got free entry all night, as anywhere there were crowds of women, the men were sure to follow. As an added incentive for the men, promo girls with super-soaker water pistols mingled among the revellers, their weapons charged up with vodka. The promo-girls were tasked with shooting straight vodka into the mouths of any willing punter. And if that wasn't enough, we were also handing out jello shots, and we had dancing girls on the bar. At one stage, we even had Jacuzzis in the club, for the more adventurous clubber.

Every couple of weeks we would hold a special event, with either a top-name DJ or a celebrity making a personal appearance. We'd got fire breathers in and on one occasion we had a girl carrying a huge python around the club. These big nights provided a cash boost that would carry us through a couple of weeks. As soon as the numbers started to drop we'd hit them with another extravaganza. The idea was to keep people talking about the club in a good way.

Between April and August we reduced the amount owed to creditors by about 60 per cent. We were all very happy with how things were going. There was an amazing buzz about the place and any teething problems had been sorted out. The staff were enjoying working there and we had re-established a good relationship with the local community and the gardaí.

Then some strange acts of criminal damage started to occur outside the building. One morning I got a call from Mike Shaughnessy to say he couldn't get into the building as someone had put glue in the locks. The culprit wasn't caught on CCTV – it was as if he knew exactly where the system was covering. Some of the anti-social elements who had been told to avoid the club would have been very capable of carrying out such a childish act.

On another occasion the club was broken into and about €150,000 worth of damage was done. The thieves broke in during the day and stole electronic equipment, spirits – anything that could be easily removed. The club was insured but it took time for the assessors to settle the claim. The alarm on the building was connected to the security company monitoring station but the thieves were able to cut the link before the alert went out. They also disconnected the siren and they even stole the CCTV recorder. It was as if they knew exactly where they were going in the building.

Then another spanner was thrown in the works. An anonymous tipster started ringing our creditors and suppliers claiming that the club was in serious trouble and was heading for liquidation. The business was profitable, but with black-propaganda being spread about town, many of our suppliers were becoming very nervous. When the club opened, our drinks suppliers had advanced us €250,000 worth of alcohol. That sounds like a massive amount of credit, but it was only about three or four weeks' worth of stock. If the club had any less than that in the cellar, we would start running out and that is very annoying for customers. Almost overnight our credit rating was wiped out. Suppliers wanted cash on delivery, and this put an incredible strain on cash flow.

The week of the break-in, we had to work almost around the clock to ensure that we were open for the weekend. If the club had lost a weekend's trade it would have needed life support. The insurance company were very slow to process the claim so all the repairs had to be made using the club's own resources.

It would have been quite easy at that stage to lock up the place and walk away but there were creditors outstanding and they all needed to be paid. A friend of mine loaned us €20,000 to reopen the club and allow us some breathing space. He said, 'Mark, it's okay – give me back the money as soon as the insurance company give you the cheque.' In the end, the insurance company paid out just €80,000 of our €150,000 claim.

Next the club was hit by a further series of protests. Some of those protesting would link arms outside the club, preventing customers from getting in. The gardaí said they couldn't do anything to move the protestors, as they had a right to congregate on the street.

On nights when the protestors were outside, there would be just a handful of paying customers inside. One weekend the club would be hopping with over a thousand people, the next, with the protesters outside, there would be tumbleweed blowing across the dance floor. It was difficult to deal with because if the club had been given a chance it would have been a massive success. When things were working well, it was flying. If the place had been a disaster and we had made huge mistakes with the planning, it would have been easier to walk away.

Even though the club had plenty of potential, the company was in such a state by that stage that you couldn't give it away. Some of the creditors started threatening to object to the club's licence. Most of them were quite reasonable when we explained that if the club lost its licence the business was finished and there would be no chance of them receiving their money. In the end most of the creditors agreed to work with us. Even Bridgeman would have got his money back if that was what he wanted.

Luckily, I still had a core of close friends and colleagues around me. One guy in the UK was a lifesaver. All it took was a phone call and he would arrange for the best British talent to come over and appear in the club. When we relaunched after the robbery, he sent over some of his best DJs to give the club a boost. He paid them out of his own pocket and told me not to worry about it until the insurance money came through. When the cheque finally arrived he said he did not want the money and only took it very reluctantly. Support like that helped to buoy us up, and there was a feeling that despite everything, the club would eventually succeed.

Things changed dramatically after the company's solicitor recommended that security guards should operate in the club around the clock to protect the building and the contents until Bridgeman's exact role in the company was sorted out. Bridgeman was annoyed by this development and he phoned to threaten me. I hung up immediately and spent a moment trying to take in what had just happened. I was shocked at this turn of events. I knew things were bad but this was getting a little too like *The Sopranos* for my liking.

It is very difficult to threaten or intimidate me, but the way Bridgeman had been talking worried me. To be safe, I called into Henry Street garda station in the centre of Limerick on the way home from Newcastle West. The gardaí gave me an escort home just in case there was someone waiting there for me. It was unnerving to think that I needed a garda escort but I did not want to take a chance. At the time I was living in Castletroy, which is a few miles away from Carew Park and Southill. The house was on a small estate but the area was quite isolated. There was a tract of undeveloped land to the rear of the house, where an attacker could easily lie in wait. It was an ideal spot for an ambush.

I had already heard from my own sources that some crime families in Limerick had been offered money to 'give me a hiding' or to intimidate me. There was nothing as extreme as a death threat – more like a few broken bones to teach me a lesson. One source claimed the money available was between €40,000 and €50,000, which was astounding. People had been killed in the city for less than a tenth of that, and I wasn't sure if this was

a rumour that had got out of control or something
more serious

The reality of the situation was brought home
to me when, on 12 July 2008, two detectives called
to my parents' house to see me. They said they had
received intelligence 'of a threat to the personal
safety of Mark Heffernan'. Naturally I was anxious
to find out who had made the threat and why they
had made it, but the officers said they couldn't
give me any more information. They said they
had been warned by their colleagues in Dublin,
presumably the Crime and Security Branch, not to
disclose any more than was absolutely necessary,
for operational reasons. They handed me a few
sheets of paper stapled together, containing advice
on how to improve my security and reduce the
chance of something happening. There were eight
or nine pages of advice, most of which was common
sense. People under threat are advised to vary their
daily routine, stay clear of public transport and, if
possible, avoid walking. You are also encouraged to
avoid busy or crowded locations, which is difficult
when you work in a nightclub. The guards didn't
officially describe it as a death threat, but someone
had passed their sentence and they were biding their
time for an opportunity to carry out the contract.
The gardaí do not deliver such a message without

good reason, and it's not the kind of message you want to ignore. Anyone from Limerick will tell you that many people have lost their lives because they did not take their security seriously enough. In this city there are plenty of people who will gladly put a bullet in your head for €2,000. I had a brief discussion with the guards, then I signed a document that confirmed that a threat had been made, and they were gone.

My life changed immediately. I could no longer take my son to school or go anywhere else with him. If some gouger was hiding behind a bush with a gun, waiting to take a few pot shots at me, that was a chance I had to take, but I couldn't put my family at risk. It was crushing that I couldn't put Lee in the back of the car and head off with him and Gina for the afternoon like any normal family.

My mother was terrified by the news. Any time there was an attack in the city, she would instantly fear the worst until word filtered through that it wasn't me. I cannot even imagine those moments of absolute dread before she knew I was safe.

The only protection the gardaí were willing to offer was the advice contained in the few pages they gave me, so I had to rely upon my own resources. Fortunately the security staff at the club were exceptionally well trained. The Polish, Russian and Lithuanian guys all had military training and that would prove to be invaluable. One of the guys told me he had no fear. He opened his shirt and showed me the scars on his chest. He pointed to them proudly and said, 'You are my boss. These are bullet holes. I got them for my old boss.' He had thrown himself in front of a gunman to save his old employer. That is dedication to your work.

We had a major meeting at the club about my personal safety and we realised that the most dangerous time was when I left the club to go home. I could go to work at any time, but once I was at the club it was obvious that I would have to return home at some stage.

We decided that when I was going home, we would travel in a convoy. An advance party of two men would drive a few minutes ahead of the convoy and walk around my house, checking if there was anything suspicious, before I got there. Then the convoy of two or three cars would drive up to the house and I was inside in a matter of moments. It was like having a detachment of Barack Obama's Secret Service agents with me.

Despite the support it was obvious that I could no longer stay out in Castletroy. It was too far away from my comfort zone. I had to return to Carew Park because I knew everyone in the area and a strange car would be obvious. I found a house to live in around the corner from my parents' home. It was a bit run down but the location was ideal. I just needed some time to refurbish the property.

Until that work was complete, we moved into the Maldron Hotel, which is only two minutes from my parents' home. Up until this point Gina had been blissfully ignorant of the threat. I hadn't told her how bad things were at the club because I didn't want her to worry. Even when we moved into the Maldron, I told her it was just a precaution and there was nothing to worry about.

We made a lot of modifications to the house and even installed a panic room. The panic room is a secure place in the centre of the house behind a steel door. In the event of an attack everyone can hide in there until the cavalry arrives. A state of the art surveillance system was also fitted, along with several high-powered floodlights. If anyone approached the house during the night, the entire place would be lit up brighter than on a summer's day.

Soon after we moved into the house, in September 2008, my father arrived at the door looking very flustered and upset. The blood had drained from his face. He had raced up from his house, which is only about 100 yards down the road.

He told me that John Dundon had just contacted him, asking questions about the club. John Dundon was one of the major criminal godfathers in Limerick and the head of the McCarthy/Dundon crime gang. Everyone in Limerick knows the name John Dundon, although I had never met the man or had any dealings with him. In 2008 he had a great deal of power and he had a feared gang of thugs under his control. In Limerick, John Dundon's name was mentioned in hushed tones and no one would say anything critical of him in public. He had called my father on his business phone. He has the phone number printed on the side of his rubbish removal van and Dundon had thought he was phoning me.

Dundon had recently got out of jail and was on holiday in Kusadasi, in Turkey. I knew I had to speak to him before he sent someone around, so I rang him back and told him that my father had nothing to do with the club and if he wanted to talk about Newcastle West he should talk to me.

Dundon said he wasn't threatening or intimidating me. He said he wanted to ask a few questions about money on behalf of Mike Bridgeman. I explained the situation with the club to Dundon and told him if Bridgeman wanted the club he could come with me to a solicitor to sign me off the company and take it over himself. I said I'd happily give him the keys. Dundon said that I couldn't have been fairer. He sounded very reasonable but he could still cause serious problems with a simple phone call.

Even though Dundon said he wasn't calling to threaten or intimidate me, he is not someone who would make such a call simply to pass the time. It confirmed to me that the threat against me was very credible. I had to increase my vigilance and become even more aware of my personal safety.

❖ ❖ ❖

Meanwhile Joe Clarke wanted to extricate himself from the company. He had had enough hassle with the solicitors' letters, and creditors were calling him directly, looking for money owed. He would tell them that he was no longer involved with the project, so there was no point in contacting him, but the creditors would counter this by saying he was still listed as a director. Joe then wrote to the company secretary – himself – as well as the Companies Registration Office, announcing his decision to resign as a director.

❖ ❖ ❖

On Friday 25 October we had a massive night planned in the club. Jodie Marsh was going to make a personal appearance. We were paying her a fee of €4,000 and were also covering her flights and accommodation. Jodie and her personal assistant flew into Shannon Airport and I went down to pick her up.

As I was about to pick up Jodie, the company's solicitor rang and told me he was in the District Court and that there was a problem with the late night exemption. He said the gardaí were objecting to the licence. Joe Clarke's resignation had become official and this created a problem, as the company needed two directors to operate and hold a licence. He said he might be able to solve the problem on Monday, but over the weekend the gardaí could close the club if it stayed open after 11.30 p.m. This was terrible news, since we had just handed over €4,000 to Jodie Marsh.

Because my jeep had only two seats, I hired a lovely new Range Rover at the airport and drove Jodie and her assistant to the Maldron. On the road in I asked her if she was hungry and offered her the choice of an Indian, Chinese, kebabs, pizza or a burger. I recommended the Chinese as I eat there all the time. She was fine with that as long as we could bring the food back to the hotel. A quick phone call sorted out the takeaway so we could collect it as we passed the restaurant.

Kevin, who works in the restaurant, came out with the food and was impressed that I had a shiny new Range Rover. Kevin was an aspiring DJ and I'd give him the odd warm-up gig for the main event. He came out for a bit of a chat, but he was speechless when he noticed Jodie Marsh sitting on the back seat.

The Maldron didn't charge me for Jodie's room. They did an amazing job and Jodie was impressed by the attention to detail. It was far better appointed than the room I had recently spent a month in. My room didn't have a beautiful big bowl of fresh fruit, and there were certainly never rose petals scattered delicately over my bed. We had a quick chat about the evening and I left her with her assistant and the bags of food. I said I'd be back in a couple of hours and I raced home for a quick shower and dinner with the family.

After picking up Jodie from the hotel it was back to Southill to collect a friend who always helped me with anything that needed to be done. It was quite funny driving Jodie Marsh though the middle of Southill. She kept asking about the areas we were driving through, but I decided not to tell her anything about the threats against me!

There was a great deal of cynicism in Newcastle West about Jodie Marsh's appearance. Most people thought that we had brought in an imposter or a look-alike. So we took Jodie to every bar in town, surrounded by bouncers who would stop punters from getting a photograph. We dashed into each bar, Jodie drank a shot and the DJ announced that she was in town for one night only and that the only place to get a photograph was West.

We had to act quickly because the exemption had been refused and we only had until 12.30 p.m. By 10.30 p.m. every bar in the town was empty because everyone wanted to meet Jodie Marsh. The place was hopping. It was one of the best nights ever in the club. Jodie lifted everyone's spirits and it was as if there were no problems in the world. The place was heaving with paying customers having a great time. The punters were queuing up around the VIP section to catch a glimpse of Jodie. Even the women were mad to see what she looked like in the flesh. She was a true professional and showed great patience with all the people looking to meet her.

Then at 12.30 a.m. the gardaí arrived and the sergeant came and spoke with me. He said: 'Mark, I'm sorry but you've no exemption this evening. You won't be able to stay open.' Thankfully, he gave us a few extra minutes to play the last couple of tunes and finish up the night properly. We didn't want to have to turn the lights on and kick everyone out immediately. There was no trouble, but as the last customers walked out the front door it was fairly clear that the game was now over, because without a late night exemption a nightclub cannot survive.

As soon as the shutters came down I told the staff and Jodie that they could have a party. By that stage all of the drink in the club had to be paid for on delivery as our credit lines had dried up. I knew in my heart that we had reached the end of the road and there was very little chance of us having another night like that. It was great to go out on such a high with all the customers leaving after having such a good time.

While everyone was enjoying the party, the manager and I sat down and arranged for the staff to get their wages. Normally they wouldn't have picked them up until the following weekend but we thought it would be less hassle to arrange everything that evening. Luckily there was enough cash in the tills and on the door to pay them.

The party was our last hurrah – a final chance for the entire gang to have a good time. A few days later the manager called me and said he couldn't get into the club. He said it looked like the locks had been changed. The solicitor said there was little that could be done. The various disputes were dragging on and I think the landlord just wanted rid of the problem. Also, once the club had lost its licence, there was no chance of getting it back, especially as we had lost a director.

The pressure was coming from every direction at that point, While I was racing around with Jodie Marsh and trying to arrange the final night of the club, I was also waiting on a very important phone call from Gina, as she was nine months pregnant and could go into labour at any moment. The timing of our latest arrival wasn't exactly ideal, but on 28 October 2008 Gina went into labour and our second son, Alex, arrived a few hours later.

Then another issue surfaced. The company was due quite a large VAT refund, somewhere in the region of €100,000. But when the company was formed nobody had ticked the box to register for VAT. This prevented us from reclaiming any of the VAT that was spent on the construction work and on establishing the club. That VAT refund would have gone a long way to clearing our creditors. We simply had no luck.

I was very down after the club collapsed. A few of my friends came around to the house and we just had a few drinks. I normally don't do that but these were exceptional circumstances. Someone out there was looking to take my life and my dream business had been taken from me. I had spent far too much time working in the club. I was amazed the day that Gina said she was expecting, because I was spending so much time in Newcastle West. The club had cost me a fortune in cash. It had also caused an unbelievable amount of trouble and as a consequence all my other business interests had withered away. I made a decision at that point that I was going to concentrate on Gina, Lee and baby Alex.

There seemed to be no way of fixing the growing number of problems and I was sad for all my staff because they had been amazing. Self-pity is not in my nature but for those few days I was emotionally drained and deflated. A fog had come down and it was covering everything.

My father came to see me and he spoke a great deal of sense. He told me I had enough to worry about with the threats and having two young kids. He said, 'Mark, there is no point fighting for this company any more. It's not worth it; the game is over. Why would you go through the hassle of paying solicitors and accountants to fight a landlord and a few companies that went in and shafted you. All the shit this place is after bringing you – leave it. It's only going to cost you more and more money.

When you get involved in it, it's more and more money.'

With the club gone, I was virtually broke. All my cash had gone into opening the business. I had let all my other business interests slide away because I didn't have enough time to keep everything organised. I had no income and I was back living off my mother and father. I was lucky that I had my parents and some very close friends to help me through that time. I had to go and apply for social welfare. I never dreamed I would ever rely on the State for my living. I had been running my own businesses since I was sixteen and I was never short of money. But now things had changed completely and I had no way of earning. I was twenty-five and the future looked bleak. My involvement with the club had completely destroyed my credit rating, so I had no hope of getting a loan to start again.

All this along with the threat to my safety left me feeling constantly on edge. The gangs had become very devious in dealing with their prey. In some cases a friend would call to arrange a meeting and the victim would end up getting shot. The gang may have some hold over the friend and could force them to set up their pal. I could no longer trust anyone outside my closest family and friends.

One night a friend rang me and claimed that

there were three strange men outside his house. It was about 3 a.m. and he wanted me to call around. There was no way I was going to leave my house at that hour. I told him that I would speak to him in the morning. It could have been an innocent call or it may have been something far more sinister. I couldn't take the chance.

My house was now a fortress and I went into a kind of self-imposed exile. These precautions are probably the reason I am still around and the gangs haven't managed to get rid of me, but they take their toll on your sanity and put huge pressure on your family life. I even started watching the likes of *The Sopranos* and *The Godfather*, looking for tips on how to survive.

But if things seemed bad at the end of 2008, they were about to get far worse.

❖ ❖ ❖

FIVE

MONEY (THAT'S WHAT I WANT)

The Limerick gangs are absolutely ruthless and think nothing of using murder as part of their normal method of conducting business. By October 2008 thirteen people had been killed in the turf war between the Keane/Collopys and the McCarthy/Dundons. But not all of the victims were gang members.

In November 2002 the innocent bouncer Brian Fitzgerald was shot dead because of a statement he made to the guards. The McCarthy/Dundons brought in an assassin from the UK to do their dirty work. They knew what time Brian finished work and they knew where he lived. The killer, James Martin Cahill, waited in the shadows outside Brian Fitzgerald's house until Brian pulled up in his jeep.

Then Cahill opened fire. Brian tried to escape, but Cahill stayed close behind, finally shooting the innocent bouncer in the head and killing him.

Shane Geoghegan was murdered in November 2008 for no reason other than he bore a passing resemblance to a man who had a disagreement with the McCarthy/Dundons. Up to fifteen shots were fired at Shane as he walked home from watching a rugby international with friends in Dooradoyle. He was hit three times in the upper body and once in the head. The entire city was baffled in the immediate aftermath of Shane's murder, because there was no reason why someone would want to kill him. Then it emerged that a horrendous mistake had been made and that it was a case of mistaken identity. By the time of Shane's burial four days later, responsibility for the murder had been pinned on the McCarthy/ Dundons – several of whom had paid a visit to my home just a few weeks earlier.

❖ ❖ ❖

In October 2008, shortly after John Dundon's phone call, some visitors called to our house in Carew Park. I was in the front garden, sawing some wood for a new cupboard to contain the CCTV equipment that we had recently installed because of the threat.

Unfortunately the camera system had been turned off that afternoon because of the work.

As I was working, Gareth Collins, Christopher McCarthy and Chucky Pickford pulled up outside my house in Pickford's red van. I knew these lads from school but I had had no dealings with them since then.

McCarthy was speaking on the phone when the other two approached me. The conversation was loud and I could overhear most of it. He remained in the car and looked quite animated, as if the person on the other end was shouting at him, issuing orders. I heard the caller shout: 'Get out of the car and give him a hiding.' He was obviously talking to his older brother Anthony, or Noddy as he is better known. Noddy was in prison at the time, speaking on an illegal mobile phone. He was serving a life sentence for the brutal murder of rival crime boss Kieran Keane in 2003. The crime was a major turning point in the Limerick crime scene, as it was an effective declaration of war between the Keane/Collopy and the McCarthy/Dundon gangs. Despite being in jail, Noddy McCarthy was still a major influence on the crime gang.

Christopher McCarthy approached me and said he had been given word from 'inside' that I was to hand over money that was owed from the club or there would be serious consequences. These lads might not be criminal masterminds but they are certainly very brutal and capable of inflicting pain or even death on anyone who crossed them.

It was a tense situation. I was on my own against three of the gang and I didn't know if they were armed. It was common knowledge that the McCarthy/Dundons had ready access to firearms and that they used abandoned or burnt-out houses to store guns and drugs.

I told my visitors that I had spoken with John Dundon about the situation a few weeks earlier and that it had been sorted. John was the head of the gang outside the prison. I explained again what had happened with the club. They suggested that I go with them to see Bridgeman but I insisted they call him instead. One of the gang rang Bridgeman, who arrived a few minutes later in his black and yellow sex-shop car.

Meanwhile I went into the house and got some documents and solicitors' letters that proved Bridgeman had done his best to avoid becoming a director of the company. Ultimately it was Bridgeman's refusal to become a director that led to the closure of the club. Bridgeman took the documents and looked over them quickly before tearing them up and shouting abuse at me.

It wasn't the first time that I had seen Bridgeman lose the head like that. The difference this time was he had the support of a notorious criminal organisation. But I didn't want to show any nervousness in front of these people because they feed on fear.

Collins and McCarthy saw themselves as hard men and were proud of that reputation. I was feeling pumped up, too, but I was conscious that I didn't want to end up brawling with them on the street. I needed to keep an eye on all of them and watch out for any reinforcements as well. I didn't even want to turn my back on them to retreat into the house. I needed to keep focused on what was happening. I knew that the gang had been driving around the area regularly. That was why I was doing the additional work on the house to improve the CCTV system. The gang didn't know the system was disconnected and I hoped that might prevent them from taking matters further.

As Bridgeman was letting rip with his abuse, my father pulled up behind my house in his van. When Bridgeman spotted him, he said to my father, 'Fuck off, you yo-yo, and mind your own business. I could have had you and your daughter hit if I wanted to.' My father remained silent so as not to inflame an already sensitive situation. I hoped the gang were less likely to do anything extreme with witnesses around.

Christopher McCarthy approached Bridgeman and told him to calm down. After McCarthy calmed Bridgeman down they left in their respective cars. Maybe I should have gone straight to the gardaí, but I was reluctant because I didn't think they would have been able to deal effectively with the situation.

This was a massive escalation. Members of my family who had nothing to do with the club were now being threatened. They were not involved in setting the club up or in running it and had nothing to do with its failure. Things were getting out of control.

While the club was still open, I had my security team and that would have scared off the McCarthy/ Dundons. They would not know what to make of the team of military-trained Polish and Lithuanian guys. They had a very impressive presence and that had been enough to deter the gang. Now I was on my own.

I was constantly looking over my shoulder waiting for someone to shoot me. One day I was talking to my mother and it made me so angry to think of the stress she was suffering because of the threat. The situation has definitely put a feeling of hatred in me, but you have to control these

Almost 1,000 clubbers enjoying a night out at Federation, Ireland's best-run teen event.

Roy Collins and me in happier times. Roy was shot dead by the McCarthy/Dundon gang on 9 April 2009, because his family gave evidence against the gang following an earlier threat.

Opening night: West nightclub was full to the rafters. It looked like all the hard work was going to pay off.

Mike Bridgeman loved 'the girls and the boom boom'.

Some of the protestors who began demonstrating outside the club shortly after my relationship with Mike Bridgeman collapsed.

McCarthy/Dundon kingpin, John Dundon, rang to tell me he wasn't trying to intimidate me. The crime lord forgot to pass on the message to his troops.
© *Press 22*

Wayne Dundon, whose conviction for threatening members of Roy Collins' family led to my friend's murder.
© *Sunday World*

Ger Dundon was one of the gang members who attempted to abduct me in February 2010. He pleaded guilty to violent disorder following the chase and received his hundredth conviction.
© *Sunday World*

McCarthy/Dundon recruiting sergeant, Jimmy Collins (right), with his en-
forcer son, Gareth (centre), and Christopher McCarthy. All three were jailed
for threatening me.
© *Justin Kernoghan, photopressbelfast.co.uk*

Gareth Collins relaxing in his prison cell.

Anthony 'Noddy' McCarthy is currently serving a life sentence for the murder of Kieran Keane. Despite this, Noddy was able to give orders to the gang over the phone when they came to my home to threaten me.
© *PicSure*

Christopher McCarthy being led into court.
© *Sunday World*

Christopher (left) and David McCormack, AKA the Skull McGintys, who were armed with a hammer and an iron bar when they tried to kidnap me in February 2010.

Building a better future through sport. Jan O'Sullivan TD at the first Changing Lives soccer programme in 2011.

emotions, otherwise they will eat you up and get you into trouble.

❖ ❖ ❖

The gardaí may not have been prepared to reveal the origin of the threat against me, but I now had a pretty clear idea of exactly where it was coming from. After Shane Geoghegan's murder, the gardaí flooded the city with members of the Emergency Response Unit (ERU) and they set up armed checkpoints at key locations. This was good for me because transporting a firearm around the city became far more difficult because of the increased garda presence. The McCarthy/Dundons were forced to lie low as a result of the garda response and the public backlash. Several of them were brought in for questioning so intimidating me fell down their list of priorities.

Nonetheless I was certain that it was only a matter of time before a gunman made an attempt on my life. I felt I was safe in my home: it was my fortress and it was impregnable. I had to tell my eldest son not to answer the front door – no matter who was outside. I didn't tell Gina the full extent of what was going on. If she knew all the details she would worry, and I wanted to keep our family life as normal as possible. It was the one area over which I still had some degree of control, because of the additional security measures I had taken. The CCTV system was linked to the TV in the living room as well as monitors throughout the house. No one could get over the wall at the rear of the house, now that it was several feet higher. Floodlights with motion sensors provided added protection. Nobody could get within a considerable distance of the house without being detected by one of the electronic monitors or alerting the dog.

I felt safe at home but on the street or in my jeep I was in danger. I spoke with a contact, who managed to get hold of several bulletproof vests for me. Anytime I left the house I wore my Kevlar. The manufacturers claim the special high-strength fibres stop a 9 mm round fired from a handgun such as a Glock. It will also stop a .22 rifle and even a shotgun. However, if they came after me with a Kalashnikov AK47 with its higher-velocity 7.62 mm rounds, the vest would only slow down the bullet. The vests provided some reassurance, but if a gunman aims for your head, the Kevlar covering your torso is of no use.

Shortly before Christmas 2008 I sat down with Gina and asked her if she wanted to go on holiday to Lanzarote, and possibly even move to the island for good. We decided to fly out on New Year's Day to see whether life in the sun would suit us and the two boys. Alex was only a few weeks old but everyone wanted a break and some sunshine and sea were just what we needed.

It was great being away from the stress, and for the first time in several months I was able to relax and let my guard down a little. I was careful not to tell anyone in Limerick where we were going, so the gang wouldn't be able to follow.

Lanzarote is a great island, with warm weather guaranteed almost twelve months of the year. It has beautiful volcanic mountain ranges and very strict planning laws banning the kind of high-rise development that has ruined other parts of Spain. My parents and my sister Lorna followed us out and it was very relaxing to spend that time with my family.

If we moved to Lanzarote, we would leave all the problems associated with the club and the McCarthy/Dundons 1,500 miles behind us, and it was an attractive idea; we seriously considered it. I even went as far as looking at a few different bars that were for sale or lease. I met up with the island's 'Mr Nightclub', who owned most of the top spots. I could have taken over a great Irish bar there and then if I had wanted. There were plenty of business opportunities on the island, and I think some of the things I had experience of, such as the Karaoke disco, would have worked exceptionally well there.

I also went to look at a beachfront property overlooking the ocean that would have been perfect as an ice-cream parlour. The business would have been a licence to print money. There were no 99-style ice-cream machines in Spain. All the ice-cream parlours had frozen ice cream in plastic tubs, which had to be scooped onto cones. The soft vanilla ice cream with a flake on top wasn't sold. My plan was to import a couple of the machines and give the Irish and British tourists what they were missing from home. I also looked at bringing over machines for making smoothies and milk shakes.

We went as far as looking for schools for the lads. The trip was far more than just a holiday: it was a trial run for a permanent move. But I knew that the McCarthy/Dundons would eventually track me down and take a crack at me.

Also, I would have needed a bit of seed capital to get started as I had lost a pile of money on the club. But, ridiculous as it may sound, the main reason I didn't want to move was my fear of flying. I knew that if I moved to Spain I would be on the plane home fairly regularly, and I hate aeroplanes. Anytime I'm on a plane I am convinced that it is going to crash. And if the McCarthy/Dundons couldn't get me, I certainly wasn't going to let an aeroplane do their work for them.

In any case, running away wasn't really an option. I would have been leaving lots of my extended family behind in Limerick and that could have left them as targets in my absence. Even while I was living in Limerick the gang tried to get to me through my relations. My grandmother's front windows were broken in her house in Janesboro. She never had a problem with anyone in her life so it seemed clear that this was done to put pressure on me. My first cousin also had the windows of his car broken.

❖ ❖ ❖

On 22 January 2009 we returned to Limerick from Spain. While we were away the gang had been asking around, looking for information about where we were. Within a few days of our return Jimmy Collins and Christopher McCarthy called to my parents' house. My sister Lorna rang me and told me to come down immediately. My parents' house is less than a minute's walk from my place, but I didn't walk there directly because there could have been an ambush. I went out the back door of my house and walked down the laneway and across a field to approach my parents' house from the rear. My father jumped with fright when I came in through the back door.

Jimmy Collins told me that senior members of the McCarthy/Dundon gang were unhappy because I had left Limerick 'without permission'. Jimmy was a very influential member of the McCarthy/Dundons and he was responsible for recruiting new members to the organisation. He also acted as muscle and his presence was a definite declaration of intent. Collins said I had until 14 February 2009 to come up with €20,000, or we would have to face the consequences.

Collins told my father that things would get very messy if I didn't hand over the cash. Things got sinister when he said, 'We've done more for less.' Those words hung heavily in the air as their meaning sank in. Collins didn't reference any particular atrocity, but he was obviously trying to trade on his own hard-man reputation and infamy. I told them I wouldn't be giving them a penny because I didn't owe them anything. Then Jimmy Collins' son Gareth pulled up outside the house in his car and they all drove off.

This was a new development: their story had changed and they were no longer looking for the money on behalf of Mike Bridgeman.

There was less than two weeks until the deadline. With two days to go I decided that I had to go to the gardaí and put the threats on record. If I was going to be murdered I at least wanted the gardaí to have information on the new threats. That way at least they would have an immediate list of suspects. I honestly didn't think that the gardaí would be able to do anything in particular. I certainly knew they wouldn't send out hundreds of officers to round up the gang and send them to jail.

It was a major decision for me to make. I was not involved in criminality but co-operating with the gardaí can cause problems in Limerick. If you are branded a rat, you would soon lose friends and become a figure of suspicion. It could even lead to being attacked. But the safety of my family and myself had to come first.

So I went into a garda station in town and said I wanted to make a statement. A garda brought me through the public area at the front of the station and into an interview room. I hadn't prepared what I was going to say, so I started by telling them about the club and how everything had gone wrong. At that point I should have been preparing for the first anniversary of West nightclub, planning a massive extravaganza. Now staying alive was my only plan.

The gardaí listened to my story but they did not take a formal statement from me. I left and hoped that things were about to change.

When 14 February came I had already decided that I wasn't paying the gang a penny. If I gave them €100, it would have been like admitting I owed them something and they would continue to bleed me dry. So I waited for something to happen. I was trying to figure out if they would strike that morning, or if they would wait a day, a week, a month before acting. If a rocket-propelled grenade had smashed through the front window and exploded in the living room that morning, I wouldn't have been surprised. I was on tenterhooks, waiting, trying to figure out what I would do in their situation. Everything was telling me that I was going to be set up and made into an example for other victims of extortion. There was no respect among the ordinary people of Limerick for the McCarthy/Dundon gang; their grip on the community was based entirely on fear and they used people like me to intensify that fear.

Almost immediately after the St Valentine's Day deadline I started taking extra precautions. I had a few cars parked around the city so no one would be able to follow me home. I'd pull into an underground car park in one car and drive out in a second one in a bid to foil any surveillance. Even though I had gone to the gardaí, nothing had changed. They had my statement and this meant that when members of the gang were hauled in and questioned in relation to other crimes, such as Shane Geoghegan's murder, they were also asked about the threats against me. The gang now knew that I had reported them, but the gardaí didn't have enough evidence to act. It was as if the gardaí needed the gang to shoot me before they could get serious. I had no protection and going to the gardaí might even have made matters worse.

Going anywhere required a great deal of planning. I was always conscious of where I would park as I had been advised not to leave the car unattended. The McCarthy/Dundons regularly used pipe bombs and improvised explosive devices. The devices are attached to the car underneath the driver's door and explode when they are disturbed. A simple pipe bomb can be easily constructed from a length of scaffolding pole and gunpowder taken from fireworks or shotgun cartridges.

The gangs have people out watching targets for them around the clock. When they are after you, everyone in their network knows to keep an eye out. I had my own friends watching out for me, too. Whenever one of the McCarthy/Dundons came into Carew Park I would get a phone call warning me that they were on the prowl.

I didn't sleep at night. During the worst times I
had three or four friends staying in the house during
the day so I could get some sleep. The only routine I
had was that nothing was routine and I could never
do anything at the same time each day. Regular
appointments could lead to an ambush. I often went
to bed at 2 p.m. for four or five hours. I might also
grab a couple of hours during the early hours of
the morning. They could be watching you round the
clock, waiting for a single slip-up. They only had
to get lucky once; my luck had to hold up all day
every day.

❖ ❖ ❖

On 9 April 2009 the seriousness of the situation
was brought home to me in the most horrrific way.
A friend phoned and told me that Roy Collins had
just been shot dead in his father's casino in the
Roxboro Shopping Centre, just down the road from
my house. Roy was murdered because his cousin
Ryan Lee gave evidence against Wayne Dundon,
who threatened to kill Ryan after he stopped
Wayne's fourteen-year-old sister from coming into
Brannigan's bar. Wayne's sister Annabel was trying
to get into the bar in April 2004, and Ryan refused

to serve her alcohol. Half an hour later a masked gunman walked into the bar, sidled up to Ryan and shot him in the leg. Ryan stood up to the gang and testified against Dundon for threatening to kill him. The McCarthy/Dundons vowed vengeance, and five years later Roy paid the ultimate price for his cousin's brave stand.

Everyone in the city immediately knew who was behind the murder. Within a few minutes the gardaí had a massive operation underway. Word on the street was that houses across Weston, where the McCarthy/Dundons are based, were being raided. I was in shock. I couldn't believe that my friend was dead. He was a young father like me, with two gorgeous daughters and everything to live for.

The guards had sealed off the car park by the time I arrived at the shopping centre, and a crowd had already gathered. Officers were pushing back the onlookers and securing the scene with blue and white tape. Sirens seemed to be coming from every direction. People were crying and screaming. There was genuine anger in the air and a feeling of physical sickness welled up inside me. The same gang who had just murdered my friend had me in their sights.

Once again the newspapers were outraged and the politicians called for something to be done. It all sounded so similar to what happened just a few months earlier when Shane Geoghegan was murdered. Nothing had changed.

Roy was waked in a funeral home. There were long queues of people waiting in line to sympathise with the Collins family. I took my place and tried to compose my thoughts as we shuffled forward. Then I saw Roy in the coffin, wearing a smart grey suit. He always looked very smart and he took care of himself. I said a quick prayer for my friend and approached his parents, Steve and Carmel. I shook them by the hand but any words I had in my mind seemed pointless. There was nothing I could say to make it any better.

The following day, Easter Monday, Roy's funeral was held at St John's Cathedral. It was the saddest funeral I have ever attended. The great and the good of Limerick all turned out to show solidarity with the Collins family. The crowds spilled out of the cathedral and people gathered outside to pay their respects. Bishop Donal Murray pleaded with the gangs to stop the utter madness. Local TD Willie O'Dea was there, as well as a host of senior gardaí. I even saw members of the Keane/Collopy gang.

Roy was laid to rest at Kilmurry Cemetery. We all went to the Lock Bar in Limerick afterwards and I spoke with Roy's mother. She is such a lovely woman and I still don't know how she showed so much dignity while dealing with such heartbreak. As I was leaving, Roy's father, Steve, told me not to worry about anything as the gang wouldn't survive much longer. I wasn't so sure.

In the weeks after Roy's murder I kept returning to his grave to spend some time alone in silence there. I had noticed that people were keeping their distance from me because I was a target, and I suppose it's understandable that they wouldn't want to place themselves in the crosshairs of a gang who have such a contempt for human life. Sometimes it felt like they weren't just controlling my life, but the lives of the entire community.

❖ ❖ ❖

After Roy's murder the gang were quiet for several weeks while they were under the intense scrutiny of the gardaí. Again several of them were pulled in and questioned. But as soon as the gardaí reduced their armed patrols across the city, the gangs were able to move around freely and they were constantly on my back again. I knew they were actively watching the Carew Park area. Anytime I went to the shops I thought someone was going to take a shot at me. I was informed that members of the gang were patrolling the whole of Southill, driving around and parking up. They knew my house was under constant CCTV surveillance so they took up station in other locations where they could see the entrance to the estate without getting caught on camera. Every day I'd get phone calls from friends, warning me that they had seen a gang member here or there. This constant drip-feed of information kept me on my toes and meant I was never able to relax.

As a family we had to deny ourselves the simplest of pleasures. We could no longer, for instance, get a Chinese or a pizza delivered, as that would be the ideal opportunity for the gang to send an imposter as a delivery driver to shoot me in my own home. So I continued to keep a low profile to avoid any form of conflict. I never believed that the gang would eventually give up, because the intimidation was always there in the background. They were letting me know that they were just biding their time. They had waited five years to hit Roy. They could wait for me too.

❖ ❖ ❖

On 17 October 2009 I was working with my father on his market stall in the centre of town. It was about six months since Roy's murder and the McCarthy/ Dundons were still keeping a relatively low profile.

Steve Collins was doing a lot of media, keeping the issue on the front pages of the newspapers, so the gang probably didn't want to give him any more ammunition. The politicans were ultimately forced to act, and in July they had rushed through emergency legislation that they claimed would bring an end to gang culture in Ireland. The new law would make it illegal to be a member of a criminal gang, and gangland crimes would now be tried in the Special Criminal Court, where there are no juries. I paid little attention to these developments because I didn't think the new legislation would help me. To me the gangs seemed above the law.

My father had been running his stall in the Milk Market for over a decade. He can be a very stubborn man and there was no way he was going to give up his pitch because of the threats. You could buy pretty much everything and anything at his stall. He travelled around various cash-and-carry shops buying up boxes of cleaning detergents, toilet rolls and slabs of minerals. He bought items with damaged packaging or short-dated tinned food that could not be sold in a shop, but that were perfect for a discount stall. Limerick bargain hunters loved it.

My father would go down to the market at 4.30 a.m. to set up his stall when people were only coming home from the nightclubs. The market finishes up around 3 p.m. but it is a very busy day, almost like three days' work crammed into one. I continued helping my father because I didn't want to let him down and leave him on his own in the market. Setting up the stall in the morning made me nervous because the Milk Market was very open. Working there was risky as it was the only time of the week when I was guaranteed to be in a certain place at a particular time.

That morning I saw a heroin junkie walking across the end of the street, carrying two black bags. He looked very suspicious as he staggered through the square. He dumped his two bags on a pile of rubbish near my father's stall. Something about the situation didn't look right to me. I couldn't think of any reason why this junkie was hanging around the market that early in the morning.

The junkie's behaviour put me on edge for the day. I was like a meerkat keeping an eye out for anything suspicious. I could have left the stall and gone home but that would have been letting the gang win, so I stayed and did my day's work.

At around 11.30 a.m. I dropped my guard a small bit. I had to go on a quick errand and was away for about ten minutes. The woman on the neighbouring stall asked me for a quick hand to help her pack away some of her goods. Her husband was away for a while and she was stuck. I didn't want to appear rude, so I agreed to help the woman. When I looked up after a few minutes three people were standing over me.

Jimmy Collins and his son Gareth glared down at me, shouting that if I didn't hand over €10,000 in a week, I was a dead man. Christopher McCarthy stood slightly away from the other two with his hand in his jacket pocket, trying to suggest that he was carrying a gun. He was playing mind games with me, keeping me guessing as to whether he was armed or not. I was focusing on McCarthy because I thought he was the greatest threat. If he pulled something from his pocket, I needed to be able to duck or run to safety. As soon as they heard the shouting, most of the other people in the market backed away from the scene. They probably thought that the shooting was about to start any minute.

Jimmy Collins said if the money wasn't handed over they would burn my family out of Limerick and take every jeep we had. McCarthy was standing very still but Gareth Collins was bouncing around like a hyped-up monkey. Gareth came up and started shouting directly in my face. He grabbed me and head butted me, narrowly missing the bridge of my nose. I pushed Gareth away and Jimmy roared, 'You are a hard man; you are a fucking hard man!'

Gareth then challenged me to a fight in the middle of the market. There was no way I was going to get into a brawl in the street with the three of them. I just kept telling them that I didn't owe them a penny, but they were not listening.

Eventually, satisfied that they had got their message across, they turned to go. As they were leaving, one of them shouted that they would be back later, but this time they would be armed. They were absolutely shameless. They made a threat like that in full view of a group of people on a busy street on a Saturday afternoon. They were convinced no one would dare stand up to them after what happened to Roy Collins.

We packed up and went home after that.

A few hours later a friend of my father rang him and said Jimmy Collins was standing beside him. The friend said Jimmy would forget about everything if I didn't report the attack to the gardaí. Reality had dawned and they realised that they overstepped the mark by attacking me in front of so many witnesses. Had they forgotten that there were CCTV cameras all over the market?

I spoke with my father and he felt that I should probably let it slide. I didn't trust Jimmy Collins for a moment but I decided not to go to the gardaí as I didn't see how it would help matters. They had done nothing the last time I tried to make a statement; why would this time be any different? The gangs had the run of the city and there was nothing that could stop them.

SIX

DEEPER AND DEEPER

It was now more than twelve months since the club had closed and there appeared to be no end to this terror. Jimmy Collins had claimed he would call off the dogs if I stayed clear of the gardaí, but he's not the sort of man you take at his word. My counter surveillance regime continued and had become second nature by this stage. It was no way to live your life, but unless I wanted to give up, it was my only option.

Just after lunchtime on 17 February 2010, I pulled up outside the post office in Garryowen to pay my phone bill. It's on a busy street, just around the corner from the Milk Market, where my father has his market stall. The road is narrow, so I parked the jeep up on the pavement to allow other traffic

to pass. I was afraid to park any distance from the
post office or in a car park: it just wasn't safe for
me to do that any more. There were people queuing
up outside, waiting for the shutters to be pulled up,
so I sat behind the wheel, hoping I wouldn't have to
wait too long. I'm lucky I decided to stay in the jeep.
Had I joined the queue or had the post office been
open, it's unlikely I'd be around to tell this story. I
wouldn't have spotted the gang when they pulled
up, and my next appointment would probably have
been with the State Pathologist, down some lonely
laneway on the Limerick/Clare border.

The gangs have plenty of pennyboys who act as
runners, couriers and spotters. It wouldn't take long
for a tip-off to reach the gang, and once they knew
where to find me, I could be guaranteed they would
waste no time doing exactly that.

As I sat in my Toyota Land Cruiser, waiting
for the post office to reopen after lunch, I kept the
engine ticking over. I noticed that the low-fuel light
was on and made a mental note to get diesel after I
had finished my business in the post office. Around
about then a blue Volvo pulled up beside me, with
Gareth Collins behind the wheel. I immediately
noticed that he was wearing a pair of black gloves.
This is never a good sign. It may have been February,
but I don't think he was wearing gloves to keep his

hands warm. Sitting beside him in the passenger's seat was Ger Dundon. That was worse again. In the back of the car I saw the two Skull McGintys and a third person I didn't recognise.

As soon as the Volvo came to a halt, the back doors flew open and the two Skull McGintys jumped out and ran towards my jeep. They were coming for me and they didn't look like they were going to invite me for tea and biscuits. I knew something was wrong so I threw the Land Cruiser into gear and drove off. There were plenty of witnesses outside the post office but I knew that people who would salute you every day on the street would suddenly forget they had seen you when the guards called round. They might feel sorry for you and sympathise with your family, but they know if they step forward, they'll be the next person in the firing line, and you couldn't blame them for keeping quiet.

As I headed up the road, there was a car coming straight for me, blocking my escape route, and I was forced to turn right, even though I knew I was driving into a dead end. I tried not to panic; if I lost the head I was finished. I accelerated down to the bottom of the cul-de-sac, swung the jeep around and reversed a small bit to give myself a bit more breathing space. I was gripping the steering wheel hard. The adrenaline was pumping and my heart was beating out of my chest. I certainly felt alive – and I wanted to keep it that way. The jeep was in gear, ready to go. I just needed a little time to work out a plan. It was like something out of a movie, but it was very real.

Collins stopped his Volvo at the end of the road, blocking the only exit from the cul-de-sac. The McGintys and Dundon jumped out and ran towards me. Meanwhile Collins walked around to the back of the Volvo and opened the boot. He stood there and watched as the others advanced on me, certain they had blocked my escape route. Dundon was waving his hands at me. One of the McGintys had an iron bar in his fist and the other had a hammer.

They were seconds away from me and I was running out of time. Their car was blocking the road, but there was still a little space on the footpath. I didn't know if the jeep would fit through the gap but it was my only chance of escape. I put my foot to the floor and heard the tyres screech as the jeep leapt forward.

Ger Dundon and the two McGintys were right in front of me. They got out of the way just in time, jumping over a wall and into someone's front garden. There was no way I was stopping, and at that point I was prepared to mow them down if I had to. It was kill or be killed.

I got the jeep up to a good speed and pulled it up on the footpath. I set my sights on the gap and prayed to God I'd fit through. I made it with a couple of inches to spare and sped out onto the street. Luckily there was no oncoming traffic, so I turned right. Going the other way would have brought me back into the centre of the city and I couldn't risk getting stuck in traffic. I was thinking as fast as I could, trying to figure out a way to safety. I decided to drive through the heart of Keane/Collopy territory. I reckoned the McCarthy/Dundons might not risk entering their arch-rivals' turf. I flew past the Garryowen shrine, with Kieran Keane's house on my right, hoping that they didn't want me enough to risk their own lives. But when I looked in the rear-view mirror I saw the blue Volvo, still coming after me. It looked like they were determined. I quickly glanced at the dashboard, where the orange low-fuel light was shining brightly. The jeep was running on fumes now. I needed help – quickly.

I picked up my phone but I fumbled trying to unlock it, and it slipped out of my hand and fell into the passenger foot well. I needed to get to Roxboro Road garda station but I knew that if I turned right out of Garryowen, I'd get caught in traffic, so my only option was to head out the Dublin Road and take a longer route that would allow me to keep

moving. I knew that if I stopped I was a dead man.
When I got to St Patrick's Road, near the Parkville
Court Hotel, there was a line of cars ahead of me and
the traffic lights were red. I pulled into the middle
of the road, dropped down a gear and floored it. The
Volvo was gaining on me, so I had to tear down the
white line and break the red light. This wasn't the
time to be worrying about penalty points. The other
drivers must have thought I was crazy. I sped past
at least fifteen cars, hoping a pedestrian wouldn't
step into my path and end up under the jeep. I knew
I was endangering lives but I was in fear for my
own. The diesel situation was getting critical. I was
playing fuel-light lottery with my life, and I was
trying to fish my mobile phone up from the floor
without killing myself or anyone else.

As I was approaching the Parkway Shopping
Centre, the traffic started backing up again. I
swung onto the wrong side of the road and steered
straight for the roundabout. I powered up over the
kerb and across the grass, hopping off the far side
of the roundabout, trying to save every possible
second. I knew the Volvo wouldn't get over the
roundabout and it might give me some small
advantage. Every metre I put between us increased
the chance of my survival. I took the road that led
past T.K. Maxx and Homebase, where there were

no traffic lights and little chance of traffic.

I finally managed to grab my phone and call the guards. I was continually changing gear to get every ounce of power from the jeep, and it was very tricky to talk on the phone, steer and stay in the right gear, while keeping an eye on the Volvo behind me at the same time.

I told the guards exactly who was in the Volvo so they knew it was serious. I was heading towards the Groody Road and I warned them that I was then going to head across to the Ballysimon Road. It was all clear in my mind at that stage. I needed them to intercept the Volvo before I ran out of fuel and was left stranded like a sitting duck. All I had to do was keep going and hope I had enough diesel to last me.

The buildings gave way to trees and fields as I headed out of the city. I was trying to lead them on a loop around the outskirts of Limerick, hoping that the gardaí could lay a trap for them. It was a bit of a risk, but I was gunning it hard, keeping up a speed of 120 km/h and I didn't think they could catch me as long as I had fuel. But when I glanced in the rear-view mirror, they were closing in on me. My heart was pounding and sweat was dripping down my face. I was trying not to lose control and end up ploughing into a tree. No matter how fast I went, I couldn't lose them.

At the next roundabout I wanted to go right. Instead of keeping to my lane like you would in your driving test, I cut the corner and sped through the roundabout, narrowly missing a car. I had no other option, as the Volvo was right behind me now. I dropped down a couple of gears and the tyres struggled for a grip on the tarmac. The jeep was rolling like a ship on a stormy sea as I slammed my foot hard on the throttle, listening to the turbo whine before quickly changing up a gear to keep the power coming. I felt like the Stig doing a flying lap on *Top Gear*, only I was driving for my life.

About thirty seconds later I heard sirens. I looked in the rear-view mirror and saw the first squad cars catch up with the Volvo. The guards pulled Collins over but I could only see uniformed officers and I knew that they wouldn't be carrying guns. The McCarthy/ Dundon gang have no respect for the gardaí and they could easily have made a call for reinforcements of their own. I knew there could be a second car full of gang members on the way. There was no way I was stopping until I felt safe. I continued up the middle of the road, straddling the white line. The fact that they had followed me that distance, and through Keane/ Collopy territory too, proved they really wanted me, so I wasn't going to relax and make a mistake when I was nearly home and dry.

It wasn't until I drove into the car park of Roxboro Road garda station and walked through the front door that I breathed a sigh of relief.

Without even taking a second to compose myself, I walked into the station and said I wanted to make a statement. Perhaps naively, I thought reporting several members of a major criminal gang would have caused at least some excitement. But the detective I spoke to said he didn't want to take a statement from me yet, although he would listen to my story. As I went through all the details of what had happened over the previous couple of years, he nodded occasionally and took it all in. The process seemed to take an age. Eventually, the garda told me that making a statement against the McCarthy/ Dundons was a very dangerous thing to do. He said the car chase might only get them a short sentence and he asked if I really wanted to put myself and my family through the strain and stress of a trial for such a weak outcome. This was a crushing blow because if things had worked out differently half-an-hour earlier, I could be dead. I wanted the guards to act and do their job. I was 100 per cent certain now that if this situation continued, I was going to be killed. I had been a victim of crime but the gardaí were essentially advising me to do nothing and they were saying there was little they could do either.

I left the garda station, stunned and confused. I had assumed that the phones in garda stations across Limerick and all the way up to HQ in Dublin would be red hot with the news that someone was prepared to testify against the McCarthy/Dundons. Instead I felt that I was a troublesome inconvenience looking to upset the apple cart.

It was as if the gardaí were not interested in my story because I had managed to escape. Would they have preferred me to be tortured so they could level more serious charges against the gang?

I crossed the forecourt, sat into my jeep and drove across the road to the filling station and topped up the diesel. I sat behind the wheel of the jeep to try and comprehend what exactly had just happened. The gang had shown once again that they were determined to get their hands on me and each incident was getting progressively worse. From my perspective it was not a question of *if* they were going to shoot me, but *when*. If things kept escalating it was inevitable that firearms would soon be used. As I drove the short distance home I thought that, with enough planning and organisation, it is possible to kill almost anyone. As I turned into Carew Park I saw a squad car parked across the road from the house. They must have assumed that the incident had begun at home. Within an hour word of my lucky escape had gone around the town and lots of family and friends came to see me and make sure I was okay.

The chase had shaken me. There was far too much luck associated with my escape. I needed to become even more security conscious because that had been too close a call.

At least it proved that I wasn't being paranoid about my security. I don't know if the gang had been lucky and spotted me passing and decided to move in on me, or if they had been tipped off by some underworld source.

Now things had moved to another level and the State was not even vaguely interested in my predicament. I didn't even have a panic button linked to the nearest garda station in case there was an attack on my home. I was expected to dial 999 like everyone else. I felt abandoned.

But what I didn't know was that phone calls were in fact being made between senior gardaí in Limerick and Dublin at that very moment, and that the Director of Public Prosecutions (DPP) was taking an interest. The DPP was looking for a test case for the new anti-gang legislation, and from that perspective the timing of the McCarthy/Dundons' latest attempt was perfect.

The guards contacted me and asked me to go

to Henry Street garda station to make a formal statement on 6 March 2010. The guards scared the living daylights out of me and said that it was only a matter of time before I was killed.

Then on 22 April I got a phone call from a senior garda, who asked me to come in immediately to Henry Street garda station in the city centre. I was ushered through the busy public office and into the heart of the station. I followed the garda up the stairs to the top floor, into a large office where the top brass were sitting around a table. This was the nerve centre from where the gardaí were running the war against the gangs in the city.

I was asked to take a seat and a senior officer spoke to me. He said the new criminal justice act that had recently been passed in the Dáil outlawed membership of a criminal gang. According to him the intimidation I was facing on a daily basis should be sufficient to send several members of the McCarthy/Dundon gang to prison for quite a lengthy stretch. The guards felt my case was the ideal opportunity to try out the law for the first time.

The officer said the force was very excited about the new legislation. Earlier laws had made it illegal to be a member of a terrorist organisation but there was nothing to prevent gangsters from organising or associating with each other. Under the old regime, senior gang members could avoid prosecution simply by not making direct contact with drugs or firearms. It was very difficult for the gardaí to prosecute if the criminal wasn't caught red handed. This new law, according to the gardaí, would rebalance the scales of justice.

I was pleased that these top gardaí were confident that the senior members of the McCarthy/Dundons were going to be jailed.

They told me that there was no chance of gang members interfering with a jury because the trial would be held in the Special Criminal Court, which is presided over by three judges and has no jury.

There had been a dramatic change in the attitude of the gardaí since I last tried to report the gang. Having previously told me that making a statement was barely worth my while, they were now saying I was a dead man walking and that eventually the gang would succeed in whacking me if I didn't help them secure convictions. It was a hard-sell technique and the sudden change of tack had me a little confused.

I was also worried about what people would think of me for involving the gardaí. I didn't want to be branded a rat or an informer. I wasn't a criminal and I had never been involved in crime but there is a genuine reluctance in working class areas to help the gardaí and I was very aware of that. But the gardaí were very persuasive and I knew that the McCarthy/Dundons were never going to give up.

The guards admitted that since the Dundons had returned to Limerick from England in 2000, the city had spiralled almost out of control. They said I had great power and that I could put everything to bed by standing up to the McCarthy/Dundons. They actually said that I could bring peace to the city. It was all so dramatic that I didn't know what to think.

The guards said they wanted to act immediately. If I got on board I would be offered protection and the chance to move abroad under a new name. The guards told me about several gangland murders in Limerick and said that no matter what the McCarthy/Dundons said, you could never trust them. This was hardly news to me. I thought about my friend Roy Collins and what had happened to him and I knew I didn't want to leave my sons without a father.

I was stunned by all the information that I had been given during the thirty-minute meeting. I wanted time to digest everything and consider my options. I was hoping for a couple of weeks or at least a few days to think about things, but I was told I had two hours. They didn't tell me then, but at that very moment hundreds of gardaí were being briefed, and specialist units were travelling from

Dublin to kick down doors across the city.

I went to my parents' house and sat at the kitchen table with my mother and relayed the conversation I had just had in Henry Street garda station. My mother was emphatic. She wanted me to help the gardaí destroy this gang that had been a blight on the city for almost a decade. I made my mind up there and then: I would put my head above the parapet. I told her, 'Fair enough. I'll do it.'

My father returned with me to Henry Street as he had a few questions he wanted to ask the guards. He was concerned about what would happen to me and what exactly was expected from his family. He also wanted to know how the guards could guarantee our safety.

After another short meeting I told the gardaí I would help them on the condition that my aunt and uncle were moved out of the McCarthy/Dundon-controlled Weston area of the city. I was afraid that because they are neighbours with many of the gang members that they would face threats and intimidation. The gardaí said they would do everything possible to get them moved, but they are still in Weston today. Concrete blocks have been thrown through their windows and their cars have been damaged in the driveway.

If I was killed before the court case, the gang

would likely escape prosecution, so shortly before I left Henry Street, I was told that two armed officers would follow me everywhere from then on. An unmarked squad car with two officers would sit outside my house and I would have garda protection twenty-four hours a day.

I was told that I was probably a candidate for the witness protection programme. They didn't have the full details at the time as a specialist unit in Dublin deals with the scheme. I would be offered a new identity and a new life in Australia or Canada, but that didn't appeal to me in the slightest because I am a Limerick man. I was born here, I grew up in the city and at some stage, hopefully in the far distant future, I will die in Limerick. I knew I couldn't walk out on my family and friends, leaving behind my mother and father, my sister and my extended family to deal with the gang while I ran away to a new life. Also, I love Limerick; it's my home and I didn't want to be forced into exile on the far side of the world.

After the briefing I spoke with my father alone, and we decided I would agree to be a State witness and help the guards take their shot at breaking the gang.

The following morning local garda search teams, backed up by the Emergency Response Unit (ERU) and the National Bureau of Criminal Investigation (NBCI), swooped on addresses across the city and arrested nine suspects. In the early hours of the morning, gardaí busted through doors and stormed the houses of many of the key gang members. The city was buzzing with the news. The radio news reported that the suspects had been moved to garda stations across the city and county. I must have been the only person in the city that morning who wasn't surprised at the breaking news. I took a great deal of satisfaction from knowing that the raid was happening because I was willing to do my duty.

The raid was the only topic of conversation that day and people were quietly hoping that for once the gangs would be dealt with effectively. Many had given up hope of ever ridding the city of the criminals, but the arrests brought some hope to the situation.

Initially, after the raids, the gardaí wanted me to move to Athlone. They had a house ready for Gina, the boys and me. They said it would be far simpler if I moved out of the city and kept my head down until the time of the trial. They were genuinely concerned that the gang were going to make an attempt on my life.

I didn't know anyone in Athlone and I felt I would be at greater risk in a town where I was a stranger.

In Limerick I know most people and who they are connected to. That intelligence was essential to my survival. I knew I would find it very difficult to settle anywhere else and build up relationships because I would always be suspicious, constantly looking for the ulterior motive.

I was even offered a free summer holiday for a couple of months. Anything to keep me happy and breathing until the trial. But I didn't want to take a free holiday and then have that used against me at some stage in the future. I didn't want to be seen as a puppet for the gardaí and I certainly didn't want people to think that the only reason I was standing up for myself was to get a few free weeks in the sun.

The only reason I agreed to be part of this process was to bring down the gang. I was doing this for my family, for the wider community and for the victims who had gone before me. I was also doing it for the next generation of kids, the lads who would be going to school with my two sons.

It didn't take long for news of my role in the arrests to hit the streets. Once the questioning began in the various garda stations it was obvious to the gang members that I had stepped forward. I was expecting some sort of negative reaction once the news leaked out, but the vast majority of people felt I had done a great thing. People came up to me and offered warm congratulations. Thankfully, nobody saw me as a rat or a snitch; instead they thought I was brave. They knew it would have been far easier to run for safety and leave Limerick behind. That would probably have been the more sensible choice.

I hadn't asked for round-the-clock garda protection but the guards said it was necessary as a deterrent. Initially, the protection officers were brought in from Cork but eventually they were replaced by local gardaí. All day and all night I had a garda escort. They sat outside my house or followed me in their unmarked squad car if I ventured out of the house.

An unmarked squad car is about as unobtrusive as a bright-pink neon sign. It might be a normal colour and not have the word GARDA emblazoned large upon the side, but to the trained eye it is easily spotted. Most have three tell-tale stubby communications aerials on the roof. Others also have special lights on the bumpers that look different from those of a standard car. These lights are activated when the car is responding to an emergency call. There is also another light fitted to the windscreen. Once you are aware of these subtle differences, these cars stand out like a sore thumb.

On one occasion I was at a shopping centre with my garda escort and one of them went off to arrest a shop-lifter. A security officer in the store had stopped a suspected thief and one of my gardaí went to attend to the incident. That didn't fill me with confidence. If they were that easily distracted it wouldn't take much of a diversion to remove them from the situation and leave me exposed. Maybe I had spent too much time watching Al Pacino in *Scarface*, but to get to know your enemy you have to get into their mindset.

On another occasion I went visiting friends and my protection detail checked the tax and insurance on all the neighbours' cars. Understandably I was told that I was no longer welcome if I had my garda friends with me. I understand that they are gardaí, but when they are protecting me, they shouldn't be looking out for tax and insurance on cars and doing their best to alienate me from my friends. Normal everyday tasks become difficult when friends and family are reluctant for me to visit because their next-door neighbour mightn't have a valid tax disc.

People also felt nervous when they noticed the protection. Instead of making them feel safer they thought there was a crazed gunman waiting for me behind every wall.

I thought the protection would have made it easier for Gina and me to enjoy a night out. But how could we go to a restaurant or to a club with two gardaí sitting a few feet away, overhearing every word we said?

Living like that and suddenly being so conspicious took an awful lot of getting used to. I had spent more than a year trying to keep as low a profile as possible to prevent any attempts on my life. If I went into a café for a cup of coffee my minders would park in front of the door and watch my every move. It was almost like sticking a banner outside saying 'Mark Heffernan is in here'. I wanted to get back to work but conducting business was impossible because people treat you differently when you are under garda protection: they are cagier and more reserved. It is tremendously difficult to act normally with Bodie and Doyle sitting outside reading a newspaper while you're trying to do business. The two gardaí might have been there for my protection but people immediately think that I must have done something wrong in the first place to be in this situation.

And DJing was certainly a non-runner. The protection detail would have had a heart attack if they had to protect me in front of 1,000 people at a venue.

The protection team needed to know in advance if I was going anywhere so they could arrange a shift change if necessary. I think they would have been happiest if I simply locked the front door of the house and didn't emerge until the trial.

It became very intrusive. My life was no longer my own and every detail of it was being documented. I had lost every vestige of my privacy and there was a feeling that the gardaí were doing me a massive favour, when in fact it was they who came to me, looking for me to make my statement and act as a witness.

That said, the protection did eliminate the threats and intimidation, which was a huge relief. But the cost of that assurance was massive. You have to put your life on hold to a great extent.

At least with a March 2011 trial date there seemed to be an end to the ordeal in sight, when life could hopefully get back to normal.

❖ ❖ ❖

Meanwhile the legal process was grinding along slowly. By October 2010 seven of the gang members and Michael Bridgeman had been charged with a range of offences. Ger Dundon was charged with violent disorder, following the car chase on 17 February 2010. Michael Bridgeman was accused of threatening to kill or cause serious harm and of demanding money with menaces. Chucky Pickford was also charged with demanding money with menaces. The Skull McGintys were both charged with violent disorder following the chase. Jimmy Collins Snr and his son Gareth were charged with demanding money with menaces and with threatening to kill or harm me following the incident at the Milk Market in October 2009. Christopher McCarthy was charged with threatening to kill and with demanding money with menaces.

The trial was slated for March 2011 in the Special Criminal Court in Dublin.

When the charges were brought against the eight men, the first thing that occurred to me was that none of them was charged with membership of a criminal gang. I had agreed to testify so that the gang members could be charged under the new legislation, and hopefully be put away for a very long time. When I asked one of the gardaí dealing with the case why the new law wasn't being used, he told me the legislation was useless. The garda said, 'We wanted to charge them with membership of a criminal gang, but our advice was that we wouldn't get a conviction. This was the first time the legislation was going to be used so we needed a conviction. But if we couldn't prove that the McCarthy/Dundons were a criminal gang, then

we'd never be able to prove any gang existed.'
This was hugely disappointing.

The guards remained confident, however, that
they would be able to secure a conviction under
older legislation, which would still mean a fairly
long stretch behind bars. I hoped they were right.

❖ ❖ ❖

I was facing into my second Christmas under threat
and it was taking its toll on our family life. I couldn't
even take my sons down to the shopping centre to
see Santa. I felt it was terribly unfair for the two
boys. I should have been able to allow them out onto
the green in front of the house to play on their bikes
or kick a football around, but we couldn't take that
risk. Even though I had the garda protection I still
refused to drive the kids anywhere or even be in the
same car as them. After the chase I realised that my
most vulnerable time was when I was driving. These
gangsters could easily pay a junkie to crash into the
side of my jeep at a junction. A heroin addict would
do virtually anything to secure his next fix, without
any consideration of the consequences.

I had to focus on making it as far as the trial
and hoping that justice would take its course. For
me, justice wasn't just putting the gang members

behind bars, it was being able to get back to living an ordinary life. I wanted to be able to work for a living and raise my children in peace and relative obscurity. I prayed that the trial would eventually bring an end to this purgatory.

❖ ❖ ❖

Shortly before the club closed the Criminal Assets Bureau (CAB) raided the place. The raid was part of Operation Platinum, which was targeting gangland activity in the mid-west. CAB had become interested in the club after an unknown source told them it might be worth their while to look into a €5-million super club in Newcastle West. They raided more than a dozen locations, including my house and my parents' house, seizing documents, computers and files.

CAB wanted to know where the €5 million had come from to open a club in County Limerick. In reality our budget was around €300,000 and we had simply used the €5 million figure on our advertising to create a bit of buzz. When the officers came to my house at about 6.30 a.m. I offered them tea and coffee and let them at it. I knew I had nothing to worry about and in the end everything checked out. Just before the trial, CAB contacted me and said they would like to meet me at my solicitor's office to return my computers and documents. I had to sign to confirm that everything had been returned to me. As the CAB officer was leaving, she stopped for a moment, turned to me and said, 'You have a very devious friend. You have one friend that doesn't like you.'

❖   ❖   ❖

SEVEN

CAN I GET A WITNESS?

After the meeting in Henry Street garda station, it was clear that the gardaí were now taking my situation seriously. Someone in the upper echelons of the force had decided that it was time to put the McCarthy/Dundon gang out of business, and my situation presented them with the perfect opportunity. I went home with the secret knowledge that Michael Bridgeman and the McCarthy/Dundon gang were going to be rounded up.

The reason I had been put under so much pressure to testify was that the Limerick gardaí were going to be supported by the specialist units from Dublin. They knew they were dealing with dangerous people, so they wouldn't move in until they had the support of the Emergency Response Unit and the

National Bureau of Criminal Investigation. Once I had agreed to testify, the surveillance and planning started in earnest.

Within an hour of the raids on 23 April it was clear that almost every senior member of the McCarthy/ Dundon gang had been arrested. Only one remained on the streets and that was because he had not been involved in the threats against my family and me. It was a massive operation, described in the media as the biggest anti-gangland raid in Limerick's history. In Ger Dundon's house on Hyde Road, officers had to ram their way through a steel door on the stairs of his home, after breaking through the front door.

Word spread fast, and before long everyone across the city was talking about the raids. Neighbours of those arrested passed on snippets of information about how the gardaí smashed their way into these fortresses and carried away their targets. With each retelling, like a Chinese whisper, the raid got slightly more audacious.

Chief Superintendent David Sheahan described the raids as 'a major offensive against criminal activity in the city'. It was the lead story on the TV and radio news, and the gardaí were praised by politicians and the media. I was relieved that the raids had gone off without a hitch.

The following morning it emerged that neither a

single gun nor an ounce of drugs had been recovered from any of the locations, but the gardaí were still confident that they could bring charges and get convictions.

The gang members were questioned over the weekend in garda stations across the city. Most of those arrested were being held under Section 50 of the new Criminal Justice Act, which allowed them to be questioned for up to seven days. Earlier legislation allowed a far shorter period for questioning. One garda told me that if someone is facing eight hours of questioning, they can stare at the corner and say nothing. It is far more difficult to maintain that kind of silence for a week.

On the Sunday afternoon news broke that the detainees would appear at a special sitting of Limerick District Court, at which they would be charged. I didn't attend this court hearing because, despite my garda protection, it was far too dangerous. The security operation at the special court sitting was the talk of the town. Members of the armed Regional Support Unit patrolled the area in front of the complex.

Ger Dundon was charged with violent disorder on 17 February 2010 by Garda Brian Colbert. Upon hearing the charge, Dundon roared, 'Ye are stitching me up again.' Christopher and David McCormack were also charged with violent disorder following the kidnap attempt in Garryowen on 17 February 2010. Gareth Collins was charged with violent disorder, and he and his father, Jimmy, were charged with threatening to kill or cause serious harm and with demanding money with menaces at the Milk Market in Limerick on 17 October 2009. Christopher McCarthy was charged with threatening to kill or cause serious injury as well as demanding money with menaces. Michael Bridgeman was charged with threatening to kill or cause serious harm to my father and me at John Carew Park on dates between 29 January 2009 and 12 February 2010. He was also charged with demanding money with menaces between the same dates. Patrick Pickford was charged with demanding money with menaces.

They were remanded in custody and only Bridgeman attempted to get bail. This was refused after gardaí objected at the remand hearing. At this hearing it became public knowledge that I was under constant armed-garda protection because of the nature of the threat posed by the gang.

At another preliminary hearing, on a special video link from Limerick Prison, Ger Dundon made an obscene gesture towards Judge Tom O'Donnell by raising his middle finger. Dundon had his face half-covered with a bandana and shouted abuse at the judge, who called for the link to be switched off because of the lack of respect Dundon showed to the court.

Things appeared to be moving rapidly but I was warned that it would take more than nine months for the case to come to trial.

The eight men were back in court on 23 July 2010, when they were served with the book of evidence and remanded into custody again. The State solicitor for Limerick, Michael Murray, asked the court to send the case to the non-jury Special Criminal Court. The State did not want the trial to go before a jury because of the likelihood of intimidation.

With each step along the road I was feeling more confident that my life could soon return to normal. But the gardaí were worried that the McCarthy/Dundons might make an attempt on my life in the run-up to the trial. If I wasn't around to give evidence, the prosecution's case would more than likely collapse, so there was now an even greater incentive for them to get rid of me.

Everybody in the city knew I was the guy who was standing up to the McCarthy/Dundons. Many would offer their support when talking to me, but when they were speaking among themselves they'd say I was either mad or unlikely to see my thirtieth birthday.

For me the summer of 2010 was dominated with counting down the days until the trial. It wasn't until another court hearing, in October, that the trial was scheduled for 1 March 2011. The trial was expected to last between three and four weeks and would hopefully finally put an end to my troubles.

I didn't receive many updates towards the end of 2010. But in early 2011 I was briefed about what was expected of me and what I might experience in court. I was allowed to look at my original statements to refresh my memory and I was told that if I stuck to the truth I couldn't go far wrong.

The trial was moved to Dublin for security reasons. This was awkward for me as I couldn't stay in Dublin for the duration of the trial and had to drive up and down each day.

The Special Criminal Court is now based in the new landmark courts complex beside the Phoenix Park and has better facilities for witnesses than the old building. In the past, witnesses, defendants and their families were forced to congregate in the same area, which could cause problems and even lead to intimidation. In the new building there are separate areas for the witnesses and even for the families of victims.

A week before the trial, we were taken to have a look around the court building so it wasn't overwhelming on the day of the trial. Getting to know the ground before kick-off is a major part of winning the game.

When you think of a court, you automatically imagine an old, dark, narrow room panelled in wood with a dock and a judge perched high above everyone else, dispensing justice. This court building is impressively modern, with masses of glass and an impressive semi-circular balcony and a glass elevator. It wasn't what I had imagined at all.

❖ ❖ ❖

On the first morning of the trial we were up before 5 a.m. to shower and prepare for the trip to Dublin. I travelled up in the jeep with my father, the armed-garda protection detail following close behind us. My father was happy to come with me to offer support, and he was also one of the witnesses. Driving across the country in the early hours of the morning gives you plenty of time to think and worry. My father was driving and we had the radio on, listening to a bit of music. Neither of us was in the humour to talk much and we definitely didn't want to discuss the case. It was nerve wracking; I hadn't seen any members of the gang or Bridgeman since the previous year as they had all been held in custody, and I wasn't looking forward to seeing them.

As we approached the court in Dublin, we turned onto Parkgate Street, up the hill and through the gates into the underground car park. That was one concession the State had made to me; at least I could sit in the courtroom without the fear of finding a yellow clamp attached to the wheel of my jeep – or something far worse attached to the underside of it.

We were taken in through a special entrance to avoid the attention of the media camped outside. We were told about the processes and what would likely happen in the week ahead. All the accused, apart from Michael Bridgeman, had contacted the DPP before the trial and said that they intended to plead guilty to the lesser charges. The guards were delighted with that and the DPP dropped the charges of threatening to kill. If someone pleads guilty there is no need for a trial and the judge will sometimes hand down a more lenient sentence. So Christopher McCarthy, Jimmy Collins and his son Gareth pleaded guilty to demanding money with menaces. Christopher McCormack and Patrick 'Chucky' Pickford also pleaded guilty. The judge said he would wait until the end of the trial to deal with their sentences. David McCormack and Ger Dundon had both pleaded guilty to violent disorder and had already been sentenced to five years for their role in the car chase.

If Bridgeman pleaded guilty it would all be over almost immediately. I wouldn't even have to testify. That would have been ideal because my family and I had suffered for long enough and the prospect of a month-long trial didn't appeal to me at all. I was committed to seeing this through but anything that made it easier would be more than welcome.

In the Special Criminal Court the three judges sit above everyone else, almost as if they are on stage. In front of them, sitting at two tables, are the prosecution and defence counsels. The barristers speak a strange language that bears a passing resemblance to English, but it is very different from the language of Carew Park. The building might have been state-of-the-art modern but what goes on inside the courtroom is definitely from an earlier age. You would almost expect to see someone in the corner scribbling notes with a quill into a dusty leather-bound notebook.

On television, courtrooms are always dramatic places with lawyers jumping up with objections and impassioned statements followed by emotional collapses after someone is tripped up on the stand. The reality of an Irish courtroom is somewhat different. The barristers keep referring to each other as their friends and the giving of evidence is a long, drawn-out affair. It's not exactly riveting stuff and you would wonder why people come into the public gallery to watch the proceedings.

The only person left to plead was my former business partner Mike Bridgeman. I hadn't seen him in over a year and he looked very respectable in his smart shirt and trousers when I saw him in the courtroom. He sat with rosary beads in his hands, looking considerably more pious than when he was driving around in his Underworld sex-shop car. His wife sat in the court during the entire trial and they were joined by their son and a few friends and family members.

Bridgeman sat directly opposite me but he didn't acknowledge me until I was on the stand giving evidence. Then he looked over at me in the box and sniggered, trying to put me off and throw my train of thought. My hopes that Bridgeman might also plead guilty were soon dashed when his barrister, announced that Bridgeman was pleading not guilty to all charges. There would be no easy ride. Bridgeman's trial for threatening my father and me and for demanding money with menaces would go ahead.

The prosecution counsel made their opening statement, claiming that they were going to prove that Bridgeman had threatened to kill me and had used members of the McCarthy/Dundon gang to intimidate me. The case they put forward sounded impressive but my opinion wasn't the one that counted.

It had been explained to me that the State had to prove their case 'beyond all reasonable doubt'. If the State failed to reach that high burden of proof then the case would be dismissed. The defence team only had to raise a 'reasonable doubt' to clear Bridgeman's name. It seemed to me that the prosecution had to achieve a lot more than the defence to win.

One thing that I found ironic was that none of the barristers was representing me, the victim. It's almost like the victim is incidental, an awkward logistical problem in the criminal justice system.

Because Bridgeman denied all charges, I was called on to give evidence against him. First the prosecution counsel, Paul McDermott, brought me through the events surrounding the development of the club and bringing Bridgeman in as a partner.

I told the court that I feared my life would become hell if I made statements to the gardaí about the various incidents and threats against my family and me.

I said my reluctance to come forward was based

on my belief that others who had made complaints could no longer lead a normal life and that members of the gang 'would not stop' if they learned of the complaint.

I made one mistake when giving evidence: I told them that I made my complaint a few days after Bridgeman threatened my family and me, but what I didn't realise was that the complaint wasn't recorded as a formal statement because I was too afraid to name any of the gang members at the time. The statement I made on 6 March, after the attempted abduction, was the first one that was on record.

The courtroom is a very intimidating place with the black-clad legal teams, gardaí and judges. Standing in front of a court with your hand on the bible is a very unnatural situation. I've been on stage too many times to count but this was very different. The clerk of the court gets you to repeat an oath and a stenographer sits on one side, taking down notes of everything that was said. The solicitors were passing yellow sheets of paper to the two teams of barristers, who were highlighting paragraphs in massive folders containing witness statements. Everything amplifies the seriousness of the place.

On the second day of my evidence I was cross-examined by Bridgeman's defence barrister. Before the trial the guards dropped around a copy of my statement so I could refresh my memory, but I had had no dealings whatsoever with the State solicitor or with any of the barristers. I had expected to be coached on how to answer questions, and advised on how the defence counsel would try to trip me up, but there was nothing like that.

Almost immediately Bridgeman's senior counsel seized upon the mistake I had made by not realising that my initial complaint wasn't a formal statement. I told him that I had become mixed up with the dates. It was a highly pressurised situation and there had been so many different events and incidents. I wasn't prepared to be grilled like that. This was the first time I had ever been cross-examined in my life and it was a horrendous experience. I had no idea that it was going to be that rough. I guess the guards don't tell you that beforehand in case you refuse to testify. I felt like it was me who was on trial. Bridgeman's barrister fired questions at me about the club and business in general. I didn't think this had any relevance to the threats against my family and me, but the judges allowed him to continue the line of questioning.

The lawyers had all the information in front of them, whereas I had to rely on my memory. With enough time to think I could have got everything right, but the barristers want to keep you under constant pressure and they deliberately try to throw you off balance. The gas thing is that the accused doesn't even have to give evidence in their own defence, so Bridgeman was never put on the stand and made to squirm.

One of the gardaí, Detective Garda Kevin Swan, told the judges that my life was under threat from members of the McCarthy/Dundon crime gang. It was strange listening to the story of the club being retold by these men who I didn't know and who were never there. I was very familiar with the events and wanted to keep jumping up and interrupting. They spoke about the initial success of the club and how within weeks the relationship between Bridgeman and me had broken down completely. In the one moment of humour during the trial a garda quoted Bridgeman as saying he got involved in the nightclub scene because he loved the lifestyle of 'the girls and the boom-boom'. Even the three judges had a giggle at that.

Eventually the court was told by the prosecution that Bridgeman called to my house in Carew Park with three other men and that he said he 'could have had' my father shot and my sister Lorna 'done'.

The following week, when the trial resumed, the prosecution spoke about the statements Bridgeman had made while he was in garda custody. According to his garda statements Bridgeman said he was in a state of shock after he had heard about the allegations and that he wished someone would hold a gun to his head and pull the trigger. In the statement Bridgeman admitted to having a row with me and to having a 'fiery' exchange, but he denied making threats against me, my father or my sister.

Detective Garda David Baynham said when Bridgeman was asked if he wanted to shoot me, Bridgeman claimed 'it would have happened a long time ago'. The garda said Bridegman told him he would rather harm himself than hurt someone else.

Then Bridgeman's counsel made an application to the judges. He made many of these during the course of the trial and the judges would take some time to deliberate on them. The guards told me these submissions were attempts to collapse the trial or to have the charges dismissed. Somebody told me that prosecuting a case was like building a house of cards: all it took was for the defence to knock one of the cards out of place and the entire trial would collapse.

This time the application was on the nature of the threat made by Bridgeman. His senior counsel said the threat was in the past tense and should not be used to determine future conduct and that

therefore all charges should be dismissed. He was
referring to the phrase 'could have had', which
Bridgeman used when he said he 'could have had
my father shot' or my sister 'done'. He claimed
the statement did not refer to any future intent and
as a result could not justify a conviction. He was
drawing a distinction between 'I will have you shot
in the future' and 'I could have had you shot in the
past' to say that his client no longer posed a threat
to my family and me. He was giving us a lesson in
English. Whatever about the grammar, I felt that
Bridgeman's intentions were pretty clear, but the
judges said they would consider the application.

After what seemed to be an age, Judge Paul
Butler and his colleagues Judge Alison Lindsay
and Judge Flannan Brennan came back into the
courtroom. Reading from a device similar to an
iPad, Judge Butler said my delay in reporting the
original threat added credibility to Bridgeman's
senior counsel's claim. The judge believed that if my
life was under imminent threat, I would have gone
to the gardaí and made a statement far earlier. The
fact that I *had* gone to the guards earlier and tried to
make a statement was not taken into consideration.
The guards didn't want a statement from me when I
went to them initially.

The judges did not understand what life was like

in Limerick. Stepping forward to make a complaint took a great deal of courage. Simply put, I came forward when I had run out of other options.

The court was silent as Judge Butler continued his ruling. He said he was minded to agree with Bridgeman's senior counsel that a statement in the past tense was not a threat to carry out something in the future. He said that as a result of this he had no option but to dismiss all charges against Bridgeman.

Bridgeman was free to leave the court.

The judge used more complicated language than that and for a moment I thought that they had ruled against Bridgeman's application. I couldn't understand why Bridgeman had jumped up and was hugging his wife. A senior garda came up to me and said, 'The trial has collapsed on a technicality. Bridgeman is free to leave. That's it; it's over.'

I was stunned. I simply could not believe that one simple little word could make such a difference. It seemed to me like excessive nit picking but the gardaí told me that sometimes things like this happen.

For the final few days of the trial, my mother and sister had also come to Dublin with us. None of us knew what to say to each other when it was over. Some gardaí came over to me to commiserate.

They said it was still good to get the McCarthy/
Dundons off the streets.

It was a long drive home to Limerick. I couldn't
quite grasp what had happened. The judge was
willing to accept that Bridgeman had threatened us
but he was throwing out the case because the threat
was in the past tense. The more I considered the
verdict the more angry I became. The judge made
reference to the delay in making a statement to
the gardaí, but I had gone to the guards a few days
before the Valentine's Day deadline in 2009. I may
not have made a formal statement that day but I did
tell the gardaí exactly what had happened.

I felt disappointed and betrayed after all the
promises that had been made. I was also very
angry. There was little point in trying to discuss the
legal niceties with me because I had no interest in
listening. The McCarthy/Dundon gang didn't turn
up on my doorstep by chance. I should have been
ecstatic with that result and there was definitely a
benefit for the people of Limerick, but the person
who was responsible for my woes was leaving the
courtroom without a stain on his character.

Now the court was in a position to deal with the
sentencing of the McCarthy/Dundons. The gardaí
asked me if I wanted to go back to court to see the
remainder of the gang be sentenced. They were

taken aback when I said no. I honestly didn't want to see anyone go to prison. People have asked me why I didn't want to see the gang jailed after all the trouble they had caused me. At that stage all I wanted was to get my life back. If I went back to the courtroom it would look like I was gloating or trying to rub their noses it in. There was nothing to be gained from going to Dublin to watch the gang get sent down. In fact it would only cost me time and money.

The gang members had done wrong and they were going to be punished, but I didn't want to make matters worse. They would eventually be released and if they continued to hold a grudge I would never be safe again.

I was happy enough to follow the sentencing in the newspapers and on the TV news. Chief Superintendent David Sheahan told the court that Christopher McCarthy had warned me that things were going to get messy unless they were 'sorted out'. Sheahan also repeated Jimmy Collins' claim that his gang 'had done more for less'. The Chief Superintendent stated that the nature of the threats had got progressively worse, culminating in warnings that I would be 'burnt out' and that I was a 'dead man'.

Jimmy Collins, Christopher McCarthy and

Gareth Collins each received a seven-and-a-half year jail term. Gareth Collins also picked up a five-year sentence for violent disorder and for driving the car during the car chase. The judge ruled that this jail term should run concurrent to the longer sentence for demanding money with menaces. Patrick 'Chucky' Pickford got a four-year sentence with two years suspended, because he was seen as having a minor role in the gang.

David McCormack's brother Christopher was jailed for five years, with two years suspended, for violent disorder. He was ordered to have no contact with any of his co-accused, apart from his brother, on his release. Christopher's lawyer told the Special Criminal Court that his client had no intention of returning to crime and would not live in Limerick following his release.

However, Christopher's claims of being a reformed character soon feel by the wayside. On 30 May 2010 he threatened to kill a prison officer in Limerick Jail. He was given a further nine-month sentence to run alongside his existing jail term.

In handing out the sentences Judge Butler said the Oireachtas viewed demanding money with menaces as a very serious offence. He said it was very clear that there was a campaign to extort money from me.

I found it strange that it was all about the €80,000 the gang were trying to extort from me; No one was asking why they came after me. The McCarthy/Dundon gang didn't just wake up one morning and decide I was a good target. But it was too late to worry about what went wrong in the courtroom. Nothing could change the verdict now. The only thing I could do was try to get on with the rest of my life.

Back in Limerick I was greeted as a hero. I had been anxious about how people on the street would see me after I had helped the gardaí, but the response was overwhelmingly positive. Strangers approached me to shake my hand. They were glad that these gang members had been jailed, because it improved the quality of life in Limerick.

The gardaí told me that with the gang's chief recruiter, Jimmy Collins, behind bars, the number of new recruits into the gang would diminish, and that would make the city a safer place. That alone was a hugely positive thing to come from the ordeal.

❖ ❖ ❖

EIGHT

UNDER PRESSURE

As soon as the trial ended, the gardaí asked me if I had changed my mind about leaving the country. They said it would be easier for me to get on with my life if I got out of Limerick. But I hadn't changed my mind. I wanted my life to get back to normal but the last thing I wanted was to be banished from my home.

In order to get me to testify in the first place the gardaí had implied that it was inevitable that the gang would get me. The deal was that I would co-operate with them and they would protect my family and me in return. I had fulfilled my side of the bargain and now it was payback time.

The experiences of the previous three years and of living under a death sentence had changed the way I interacted with the world. I used to be someone who was very outgoing, constantly out and about doing business. All that had changed as a result of the threats, the trial and being placed under protection. It became very apparent in the aftermath of the trial that my quality of life was not going to improve anytime soon. Attempting even the simplest of activities provided a constant reminder of everything that I had lost out on.

While I was working I was always very busy and active. I'd be up at the crack of dawn and I'd work until late at night. When I had spare time I'd go to the gym or play football. I was always doing something to keep me active and healthy. I could no longer do anything like that, and between the club closing in October 2008 and the summer of 2011, I put on almost five stone in weight. I am lucky that I don't drink or smoke. If I was a drinker, I would be a raving alcoholic by this stage. But my addiction was eating. I loved Chinese takeaways, pizzas, kebabs – anything with a tasty artery-clogging sauce.

I was eating takeaways at anytime between midnight and two o'clock in the morning. Then I spent all day in bed because I had nothing much else to do. I felt that my energy was being sucked from me because I had nothing to look forward to or work towards.

My life was supposed to improve after the trial but it was actually getting worse. I felt like whoever had control of the light at the end of the tunnel had removed the bulb. The gardaí provided me with protection but that came at a high price.

One evening I wanted time to clear my head, so I decided to go for a walk. This should be the most straight-forward of activities in anyone's life. It doesn't cost anything and you don't need any special equipment to go for a stroll. You just look outside and see if it's raining before deciding whether you need an umbrella or not. But as soon as I left the house my garda escort followed me in the car and rang me to ask where I was going. I told them that I was going for a nice evening stroll. It was surreal having an unmarked squad car creeping forward a few feet behind me. I walked towards the canal and continued along the towpath. The car couldn't fit on the path at the water's edge, so one of the gardaí was forced to get out and follow me on foot.

All I wanted was some peace and quiet to think through my future and figure out what to do with my life, but a few feet behind me I could hear an officer giving a running commentary of my progress over the radio. 'Heffernan's proceeding on foot to an unknown desitination. I don't know where he's going; this is unusual. He is still proceeding on foot.' All that was left out was which foot I was using at any particular moment.

I wanted to turn around, grab the radio and throw it into the canal for a moment's silence. It was like the constant drip, drip of Chinese water torture. If they had deliberately tried to devise a scheme guaranteed to make Mark Heffernan lose his mind, they couldn't have done a better job. With virtually every step being reported back to base, my frustration was rising. I had to turn around and head for home before I lost my temper and started a row. 'He has turned around. It looks like he's going home'.

Sometimes I felt that I would have been better off if I had been thrown into jail for two years, rather than having to put up with this disruption to my life. At least I could train in the prison gym and keep myself healthy.

And yet I knew I still needed the protection. Even though there were seven gang members behind bars, there was still a huge threat to my life. There were many other gang members still on the streets, and the Limerick gangs have been known to call on associates in Dublin and elsewhere to carry out murders on their behalf. Being in jail didn't stop them from issuing orders on illegal mobile phones.

The one gratifying thing for me was the reaction of the people of Limerick to the gang being smashed. People were delighted that the McCarthy/Dundons were severely damaged by the case. Importantly, with Jimmy Collins off the streets, the gang's main recruiting sergeant was out of action. The gang often pressurised young people in the area to become involved in criminal activities such as storing guns and drugs. Then if they were caught with the guns or the drugs they would owe the gang the cost of the losses. Very often the gang's dealers would get young kids hooked on heroin so they could fully control them. Once a kid is on drugs he will do anything for his next fix. At the height of their powers, the McCarthy/Dundons could call on up to 500 people. That figure might seem very high, but they had many people doing a broad range of jobs for them. They weren't all dealing drugs or intimidating victims. Some might have respectable jobs but would provide some form of support, like looking after a dodgy package. That person wouldn't be a full-time member of the gang but they could be called upon as needed. If they stepped out of line or refused to do as asked, they would be given a brutal beating.

If a car was stolen for use in a crime, the gang would need someone to identify a second car of the same make, model and colour to copy its identity. A stolen car will immediately show up on a garda computer if an officer checks the number plates, but a cloned car will pass a cursory inspection.

These small-time members wouldn't be expected to go out and shoot someone, but their logistical support was essential to the efficient operation of the gang and they received some money in return. With the major players behind bars, the number of these associate members began to dwindle.

The gardaí's success had another impact. 'Ambitious' youngsters joined the gangs because they saw the senior members flashing their cash and driving fast cars. But now CAB started targeting the imprisoned gang members' wheels. Ger and Wayne Dundon had imported two special BMWs from Germany at a cost of €350,000. The BMW X5 and 3 Series were armour plated with Kevlar to stop pipe bombs and bullets. They even had bullet-resistant glass. Ger and Wayne paid cash for the modified motors and even registered them in their own names. When CAB came knocking, the Dundons found it difficult to show how they had paid for the cars without any legitimate income. The cars were seized and a great many people laughed when they saw them on the back of the tow truck. Shortly afterwards, news broke that the government had

handed the cars over to the Emergency Response
Unit. There was no way that the government was
going to buy the gardaí two cars worth €350,000, so
they got them for nothing.

❖ ❖ ❖

Going outside was always a source of tension.
One time I parked the jeep outside the Meteor
shop on O'Connell Street in Limerick and ran in
to pay my bill. My protection officers parked on
the pavement directly behind my jeep. I had been
warned not to leave my car unattended for any
length of time so I wanted to keep it within sight.
I had joined the queue at the counter when a garda
came in and said he wanted to have a chat with me.
The garda said I had to move the jeep, so I told
him that was no problem. I forgot about the bill,
got back into the jeep and pulled into the traffic.
Within seconds two squad cars drove up behind
me with their sirens blaring. I thought there had
been an armed robbery until they pulled up in front
of me and the guards jumped out. I was ordered
out of the jeep and they arrested me for parking on
a double-yellow line.

They took me away in handcuffs and brought
me to the garda station. I was furious. Who gets

arrested and led away in handcuffs for parking on a double-yellow line?

I couldn't understand what was happening. I had put my neck on the line to break up a major criminal gang and now I felt I was being targeted by the gardaí. It was a crazy situation.

I was taken to a garda station, where I was processed and put into a holding cell. They even took my shoes from me in case I tried to hang myself with the laces. Within an hour everyone in the city had heard that I had been arrested in the centre of town and taken away in handcuffs. Why did they need to handcuff me? I had two armed officers following me everywhere. It wasn't as if I was going to run off.

To me it looked like they wanted to embarrass me in front of the entire city. A friend told me that they probably did it to put manners on me and to stop me complaining about my treatment.

After you are arrested, a garda has to outline your rights and explain to you in ordinary language the reason for your detention. The gardaí never bothered to do this with me. They just left me to stew in the holding cell. After about two hours I started to complain of chest pains. I said my chest was tightening up and I was becoming short of breath. Suddenly their attitude changed. They rang an ambulance and I was released from custody, but only after I signed my bail bond. I had not been charged with any offence and yet I had to sign a bond for my release.

I didn't think much more of it until the summons arrived at the house, citing me for dangerous driving among other things, all for parking on a yellow line.

Before the court date came up, the gardaí said if I pleaded guilty to an obstruction charge, they'd drop everything else. But after they dropped all the other charges, I told them I was still going to fight the obstruction charge. With everything that had gone on over the last couple of years, I had learned a valuable lesson: if the prosecution doesn't get all its ducks in a row, the case will collapse. So my solicitor sought the statement from the arresting gardaí. The gardaí complained that no statements were ready as they thought I was going to plead guilty. They said I was going back on my word.

I wanted to show that I wasn't a push-over, because this wasn't the first time I had been arrested and taken a garda station in handcuffs. For an innocent man who had acted as a State witness, I felt I was wearing their bracelets far too regularly.

On the previous occasion, I had lost my protection detail in heavy traffic. It wasn't my fault; I was keeping with the flow of traffic and had to

obey the lights. They got stuck and contacted my
liaison officer, who rang me. Then the protection
detail called my mobile. For a few minutes there
was a game of phone tennis, with calls going back
and forth between the station, the protection car
and me, so I was on the phone when another garda
pulled me over. I presumed he was going to help by
radioing the protection detail and directing them to
where I was. Instead he gave me a world of grief.
The garda asked me my name, but I was frustrated
and I told him he knew exactly who I was. At that
point I'd say every guard in Limerick knew who
I was. When my protection detail turned up I was
arrested because I refused to tell the first garda my
name. I ended up being taken back to the station
in handcuffs in my own protection car. The garda
wanted to prosecute me for using a mobile phone
while driving, even though I was talking to his
colleagues at the time.

This all happened before the gang members' trial
and, because the gardaí still needed my assistance,
I was released within a few minutes, with profuse
apologies.

Another time, I was watching a football match in
Southill. My protection detail decided to wear bright-
yellow garda jackets and stand near the entrance
to the football ground. The very obvious garda

presence was making people feel uncomfortable, so I rang my liaison officer and asked if he could ask them to remove the high-viz jackets and try to look less conspicuous. He said that wasn't possible, so I decided to leave the football match and go to visit my mother instead.

I drove to my parents' house and parked the jeep in the laneway behind. But the protection detail hadn't seen me leave and they thought I had deliberately tried to sneak out and leave them behind. They drove around for a while before returning to Roxboro Road garda station, where they parked for the remainder of their shift.

The best one of all was when I was pulled over by a guard in the presence of my own protection detail to check my driver's licence, tax and insurance. The guards don't actually need to pull over a car to see if it is taxed and insured – all the information is on computer. They can call a special unit in Ballina to access the garda PULSE computer system. They might pull over a car to satisfy themselves of the identity of the driver, but I'd hope that with my own protection detail present they knew who I was by that stage.

These petty instances made me feel that was I the criminal, yet all I had done was what the gardaí had asked me to do. I felt that I was being punished for doing the right thing.

❖ ❖ ❖

Because of the protection I was spending more and more time at home, sitting in front of the TV. I was in a situation where I had no DJ business and after everything that had happened with the club, there was no point in calling the bank to look for a loan to start a new business. Failing at something hits your self-confidence. I didn't want to sit at home for hours on end but that was what I was doing because my motivation had fallen so low. I had nothing to focus my energy on, apart from considering which takeaway menu I was going to order my next meal from.

Things eventually came to a head and I decided I couldn't remain locked up in my own private prison for the rest of my life. I needed aims and something to work towards.

Spending so much time at home and around Carew Park had made me far more aware of the problems we have in the area. Carew Park has become rundown over the years and that neglect is partly responsible for the rise of the gangs. In 2008 the regeneration project was announced and it was decided that up to 400 homes would be demolished in Carew and Kincora Parks. Huge swathes of the estates were going to be knocked down. People were angry as they felt the estate needed investment and not bulldozers.

There are some people in the area who want to move and are looking for a transfer out of Southill. They aren't interested in the regeneration or improving the community. They are looking for their ticket to the nice part of town, away from the joyriders, drug dealers and crime. I don't blame them for trying to get away but not everyone can run. It is human instinct to try and jump from a sinking ship, but there are plenty of us here who believe that Carew Park is worth saving.

My feeling is that it would be far better if the area could be renovated and improved, rather than rebuilt. The kids on the streets need youth centres and all-weather playing pitches. They need safe places where they can meet up and hang out. The street corner is not a proper place for teenagers. Even if they are doing nothing wrong, they appear menacing, and older people are often afraid when they see youths wandering around and sitting on the walls outside their homes. A new house won't solve that problem.

The young people have nowhere to go and few positive role models. So it's understandable when they see the gang members driving around in the high-powered cars that they aspire to be like them. In the absence of positive role models and worthwhile things to direct their energy into, young people see becoming a gangster as an achievement.

The kids in the area need to see people from their estates working and being successful. They need to be shown that people like them can make it. We have to provide other options and activities to keep them busy. A small amount of money spent wisely could help prevent major problems later on.

If we can change the attitudes people have towards crime then we are half way to winning the battle. Twenty years ago it was acceptable to have a few pints and drive home afterwards. Now nobody would admit to doing that. Education is the key.

With the McCarthy/Dundons seven members down, I thought this might open up an opportunity to change things for the better and make it easier to reach the kids who might otherwise have got involved in the gang. The structure of a gang is a bit like a house: when you take out the foundations the rest of the building will collapse. Jimmy Collins, his son Gareth, Ger Dundon and Christy McCarthy were like the foundations and the gang was shaky without them around. Also, word soon filtered through that Jimmy Collins had fallen out with the McCarthys and the Dundons, and that their alliance was over. The gang were rowing amongst themselves in prison, with the different factions blaming each other for what happened.

Not only were the McCarthy/Dundons having problems in their own gang, but they were still in conflict with the Keane/Collopys. Much of the feud was taking place in prison because so many gang members were inside.

Everyone in the city knows there has been enough violence and it is time to calm things down. Jailing the gang members buys time – at some stage they will be released, but there is a window of opportunity there. That's why I decided to become involved in community work, so I can give something back to all the people who have supported me. I have two children who are growing up in Carew Park and I need to think about their future too.

I want to use the experiences I've had over the past four years to my benefit and that of my community. Something constructive has to come out of everything that has happened. That is why I am so committed to my charity, Changing Lives.

Everyone involved in my case will be out within three or four years. The heaviest sentence any of the gang received was seven and a half years. Prisoners automatically get a quarter of their sentence

knocked off for good behaviour, which reduces the
jail term to a little over five years and six months.
That means all of them will be back on the streets
before Christmas 2015.

There have been attempts in the past to bring
peace to Limerick. I have been told that some of
the gang want me to go into the prison to meet
them to clear the air between us. That may simply
be an attempt to secure an earlier release date for
themselves, but I do not gain anything from those
men being in prison. I take no pleasure in their
prediciment.

I needed to re-evaluate my life and what I wanted
to do with it. I loved the entertainment business, but
it was my nightclub that put me into this situation.
Having so much time on my hands gave me the
chance to set up Changing Lives, and I can use it to
make a difference in the community.

❖ ❖ ❖

NINE

THINGS CAN ONLY GET BETTER

Since the club has closed I have had plenty of problems in my life but I am aware that many in my community are in worse situations. With all my time off I noticed that many kids are hanging around the streets of Southill with nothing to do but get bored and cause trouble. I spoke with some of them and the stories depressed me. Some begin by drinking cider, before moving on to using hash, cocaine and heroin. For many the route to criminality is through joyriding. Joyriding is a massive problem in Southill. The gangs always need someone who is able to steal a car and to act as a getaway driver, so joyriding has become a kind of gateway crime to more serious gangland activity. Good kids are going bad because they are making the wrong choices and they don't know that they have other options open to them.

The Limerick Regeneration people and Limerick City Council are both trying to work in the area but their success has been limited as there is a great deal of suspicion in the community about these organisations. The official organisations believe in an approach in which policy is decided upon by a high-level committee and then imposed upon the community. I think policies should be developed at grassroots level by the people who will live with those policies. This is partly the reason why I decided to found my charity, Changing Lives. I want us to provide an alternative to the downward spiral of crime, drugs and death, from the ground up.

I registered the name Changing Lives with the Companies Office in June 2011 and it has taken a great deal of work to bring it to a point where it can actually help people. Trying to establish a new charity is a very time-consuming business. There is an unending amount of red tape to keep you tied up with bureaucracy instead of going out and helping people.

The charity was founded to help disadvantaged teenagers and children in Limerick, to show them there is far more to life than gangs, joyriding, murder and drugs. Of course my involvement in youth work is not entirely out of the goodness of my heart – I have a selfish reason for wanting kids to steer clear of the gangs. Each new gang member is a potential assassin, so every teenager who takes the right road is one fewer threat that I have to worry about.

I want Changing Lives to be the Ronseal Quick Drying Woodstain of charities – because it does exactly what it says on the tin. The hope is that Changing Lives will be a success in Southill and then we can roll it out across the rest of Limerick and eventually run programmes nationwide. The Southill project will act as a template that can be reproduced in other areas.

To work with children you need to be vetted by the gardaí. In light of everything that has happened in Ireland, this is perfectly understandable. It is, however, a long, drawn-out process as you have to get on an official vetting list and wait your turn. In a bid to speed up things, we decided to bring Changing Lives into the structure of our local football club, Hill Celtic, and I became the chairman of the club. The Football Association of Ireland (FAI) has its own child protection officers and is already on the official vetting list. Once Hill Celtic was affiliated with the FAI, anyone working with the club could be vetted by their officials. The FAI gave us great support and provided us with the logistical support and guidance to work our way through the system. The FAI is often criticised but their support for grass roots football is unbelievable.

Hill Celtic is far more than just a football club. Of course we have a number of teams and the game is very important, but it is what the club can do in the community that is the key. We have a community development committee in the club, through which we are going to run the Changing Lives programme. Producing winning football teams is of course one of our aims, but for us, giving the youth of Southill a direction in life is the most important goal we can score.

The FAI has helped us establish a leadership course for some of the lads who have volunteered with the club. The guys are currently working on their FAI coaching badges so they can train some of the younger teams. Primarily the courses are to teach the lads how to become effective football coaches, but, importantly, that involves developing their leadership skills so they can become role models. Apart from coaching, the courses also offer the participants qualifications in first aid and as community outreach workers. They will be trained in counselling and be given the confidence and knowledge to help troubled youngsters. By the end of 2012 a dozen local guys will be qualified. If the coach does not have the appropriate skills to deal with a particular problem he will know where to go to seek the necessary help.

We want to engage with local kids and arm them with the knowledge necessary to make the correct decisions in life. We are not going to tell them what to do; hopefully, given the opportunity, they will be able to choose the right road themselves.

We already have two football grounds and we want to build a community centre beside one of them, where we can provide education through football, as well as a drop in centre for teenagers for when they get bored. Then we can build links with other organisations that deal with issues such as depression, drugs and alcohol dependence. I have found that many people in the area are completely unaware that help for their problems is available if they just knew where to look.

I have spoken with many people who were involved in drugs and crime to try and discover why they went down that road. We all know that crime and drugs are a blight on the area but hoping they will go away is wishful thinking. The drugs are not the disease; they are a symptom. There is always a reason why someone starts taking drugs and until we address those issues the drug problem will remain.

While I was conducting my research I spoke with one local guy who is the same age as me. He comes from a good family with fine parents and loving brothers and sisters. When he was growing up he was a great footballer with lots of promise and he had a great circle of friends. But on the day we met, it was clear that heroin had taken its toll on his body. The former athlete was a shadow of the man he used to be. For much of the last seven years he has been an addict.

I was fascinated by his story because his background wasn't that of what we think of as the stereotypical addict. When he was twenty-one his older brother died and it hit him incredibly hard. Until then, sport had been his life, so apart from a few pints he had nothing to do with drugs. In his grief someone offered him a few lines of cocaine to 'cheer him up'. The drugs were supplied by one of the gang's dealers. Soon he was using cocaine regularly and as his consumption increased he couldn't quite afford the amount of money he was putting up his nose. The dealer offered him a way to reduce the debt: storing guns in his house for safekeeping.

Eventually heroin replaced cocaine as his drug

of choice. At first he smoked it, and when that was no longer effective he began injecting it. He abandoned football, his friends and his family. The only thing that mattered to him was securing the next fix.

Gradually his life spiralled out of control. He told me he was self-medicating with the heroin because of the pressure the gang were placing on him. Because of his addiction he had become a foot soldier in the McCarthy/Dundon gang. The gangs have even been known to give guns to addicts to kill people for a bumper bonus in heroin.

He told me he had committed armed robberies and mugged old ladies just to feed his habit. 'I'd even kill my own father for a few euros to buy drugs. That's how bad I got,' he said.

He'd regularly commit several crimes a day and admitted that he was an anti-social menace. Jail wasn't a deterrent to him because drugs are as easily scored behind bars as they are in Southill, and the drugs were more important to him than his freedom.

He had a couple of kids with a girl around the time he had started dabbling in drugs. Once his addiction took hold, his girlfriend kicked him out and barred him from seeing his children. He said, 'It breaks my heart. Every day I see the kids as I walk by their house. I know who they are but they have no idea who I am. I want to kick the drugs.'

I arranged treatment for him in Dublin to give him a fighting chance to kick heroin. But I couldn't promise him that he would get cleaned up in rehab or that his girlfriend might let him see his kids again. Ultimately that was up to him.

His story is depressingly common. While he is on drugs he is a danger to himself and society, but we shouldn't write him off as junkie or a scumbag.

The process of getting clean is far more than removing drugs from your life; there are many mental and emotional issues that need to be resolved. For rehabilitation to work, the addict has to want to kick their habit. They also need help and support for when they feel depressed or want to get a quick fix.

When Changing Lives is fully up and running we will have outreach workers from the community who people know and trust. They will have the knowledge to help those who have developed a drug problem and eventually we plan to have ex-addicts working with us to show there is a way out.

❖ ❖ ❖

Last year we ran a major three-day football programme for 700 youngsters from the area in association with Arsenal Football Club and Limerick FC. Arsenal works with a large number of youngsters from the more deprived areas of London and it was great to get them involved and to learn from how they do things.

An enormous amount of organisational work was needed to run this programme, and the local community came out in force and did the heavy lifting. It was a massive undertaking because we had to arrange food, marquees, goal posts and even portable toilets.

The guy who delivered the toilets was afraid to leave them unattended in the middle of Southill because they contain a valuable pump. He told me that the pumps are often stolen by gangs who rob heating oil from storage tanks. He was worried the toilets would be destroyed by the time he came back. All of the equipment was in the middle of Southill for five days and nothing was damaged or stolen.

Getting the pitches ready was a big challenge. I enlisted the help of Anthony Kelly and Paul Crawford, both of whom have extensive criminal records. There was a great deal of history between the two and in the past if they were to meet, the encounter could easily end in violence. Anthony Kelly has received numerous jail sentences; if you were to add them up they would total more than 100 years. He was one of the driving forces behind Hill Celtic, but after he was arrested he had to stand down as chair of the club in 2011. Paul Crawford was a key member of the McCarthy/Dundons and had at least ten junior gang members under his control. Paul's brother Noel was murdered as part of the feud between the gangs. He was at his parents' home, celebrating his fortieth birthday with his family in December 2006, when a gunman approached the house and opened fire. Noel, who had six children, died several hours later at the Midwestern Regional Hospital. Paul was the intended victim that day, but the killer shot his innocent brother instead. Noel had absolutely no involvement in criminality.

Working together with Paul and Anthony on the field in the middle of Southill was an important statement to the community. If two former enemies could work alongside each other then there was real hope for Southill. Both men have now turned their backs on criminality and are trying to give something back to their community.

To some it appeared strange that I was working with Paul Crawford in particular, when his former comrades in the McCarthy/Dundon gang wanted me dead. But there is method to my madness. If I can turn the gang members from crime and get them involved in the community, it will make us all safer.

We needed to mark out a few pitches with white lines and cut an awful lot of grass before we could start putting up the marquees. Someone spotted the three of us working together and put in a call to the estate manager of Limerick City Council's Regeneration committee. They were expecting a war to kick off because of the history between Anthony and Paul. We were just concentrating on getting the job done. These two guys are now committed to helping the young generation avoid making the same mistakes they did.

It took us three days to fix the field, mark out the pitches and arrange everything. We even set up barbecues so we could feed the 700 hungry youngsters and their families. The conversation was about football and general things. Paul and Anthony didn't exchange one bad word.

Anthony has contacts in Limerick FC, and with their help we were able to arrange for John Keyes of Arsenal Football Club to come over for the three-day programme. John is a project leader with Arsenal in the Community and has great experience of using football to bring communities together. The programme was a major success and it created a positive buzz in Southill. It demonstrated that with a little hard work and dedication we can improve our own situation. The Regeneration people came to the event and took lots of photographs, and I felt we were showing them that regeneration was about people and not buildings.

I wanted to build on our initial success by joining the Carew Park Estate Management Committee. The more I spoke to people, the more I understood their problems. I could see solutions and I thought joining the committee would be a great way to help make a difference. But the committee rejected my application due to health and safety concerns. They claimed I was a risk to the other members of the committee because I was under constant armed-garda protection.

I decided not to get down about this and instead we used the momentum created by the football programme to arrange community barbecues, clean-ups of the area and even coffee mornings for the elderly. Graffiti might seem like a minor nuisance, but to the residents of Southill it can be a real blight. It is a sign that an area is unloved, so we bought some paint and the residents took responsibility for painting over the graffiti. We also arranged skips to remove rubbish and people used their own lawnmowers to cut the grass in public areas near their homes. Everybody's small actions made a big difference to Carew Park. It was clear that people were willing to pitch in and work to improve the estate, so I had the idea of establishing a forum where residents could bring forward ideas about ways to improve the estate. For example I would love if we could create allotments and give people the chance to grow their own vegetables. There are plenty of green areas and I'm sure there are some residents who would love the opportunity to plant a few spuds or carrots.

I arranged a public meeting on the green in the centre of the estate. For two hours before the meeting I drove around Carew Park with speakers bolted to the roof of the jeep, encouraging people to come out. A friend drove the jeep and I sat in the passenger seat, broadcasting away. I played a few tunes and then told people about the meeting, with my two armed gardaí following close behind. With just two hours' notice, between 200 and 300 people turned out to the meeting. I was quite surprised that no local councillors attended but I later heard that officials in the council had contacted them and asked them to stay away from the event. I felt it showed once again that officialdom was afraid of what we all represented.

At that meeting we decided to establish our own concerned residents group and we elected a steering committee. The first thing we all agreed on was the need for children-at-play safety signs in the area. The signs were a small thing but they showed that working together could yield results.

As this work continues there is no reason why Southill couldn't enter the Tidy Towns competition. People may laugh at that but I think it's possible when I see the pride that a bit of work gives the residents. Getting people to look after their own area and take pride in it is one way of keeping anti-social behaviour under control. If people are spending hours during the day tidying an estate they will not tolerate others coming in at night and destroying that work. All these gradual steps will improve the area without having to send in the bulldozers and razing the estate to the ground.

❖ ❖ ❖

Shortly after the football programme, John Keyes from Arsenal called us and said he was very impressed by ten of the local guys who played in the programme and he invited them over to train in London. It was a big deal, not just because one of these Hill Celtic lads could be the new Dennis Bergkamp or Thierry Henry, but because they were getting positive reinforcement for something good they had done.

A local businessman chipped in and sponsored the trip for the lads. We had a meeting before the trip and I told them not to be embarrassed about where they are from and who they are. I told them that they were representing their community and the club and to do us proud.

The ten lads played in a street-league tournament in Hackney, which is a rundown area near the Arsenal Emirates Stadium. There were a number of scouts from the club watching the tournament to see if there was any undiscovered talent. The lads were also given a private tour of the team's magnificent new stadium. The trip finished with tickets for Arsenal V Bolton Wanderers.

One of the guys on the trip has been called back to London for a few more sessions. The club seem to be very interested in bringing him over, and if that happens it will be a massive boost for Southill, Hill Celtic and Changing Lives. It will be further evidence that our system is working and producing results. A big success will provide further momentum and draw even more kids into our programme.

We've learned a great deal since we started Changing Lives. For 2012 we have great plans for Hill Celtic, including another major football programme. This time we're going to invite a

high-profile English football team in to play a
friendly in Limerick as a fundraiser.

We also want to run a youth football camp and
organise other events that will occur more regularly.
We plan to use the street-league idea that was so
successful in Hackney. Southill alone could field
at least four teams, and we could invite teams from
other areas to help break down barriers between
youngsters from what have been seen as rival parts
of the city. I believe football can bring communities
together and encourage respect.

We are going to fill a gap that has been left
by the Regeneration people. You would expect
that, after spending €150 million, they might have
provided some changing rooms or a clubhouse. We
want to develop an all-weather pitch and even an
indoor training centre so we can host games all year
round. We are going to fundraise for these facilities
ourselves because we cannot wait for the officials
to come up with the goods.

Teenagers are hanging around on the streets
and getting bored because they have nowhere else
to go. That can lead to problems, but rounding up
youngsters and jailing them does nothing to break
the cycle. If there was a drop-in centre with games,
computers and Play Stations it would help to keep
bored kids out of trouble. Teens attending the drop-in

centre would also have access to information on health matters, training and jobs. It is all about intervening at an early stage and giving the kids options before the problems get too serious.

For many teens joyriding is their first taste of criminality. Young men have a fascination with cars and engines and joyriding is the only way they can experience the thrill of speed. We have to find a way to channel that interest in cars in a positive way. If we had a place where youngsters could work on cars legally and learn a trade, before racing those cars on a properly organised stock-car track, we would be providing a skill that might secure them a good job. And the ordinary people of Southill would sleep sounder at night, knowing that their cars are safe and that they won't be woken by the skidding and squealing tyres of joyriders.

Some of the people of Southill have even approached me to see if I would be willing to run for Limerick City Council so they could have someone they trust on the inside, influencing decisions. I was surprised when the first approaches were made and I said there was no way I wanted to be a politician. The gardaí were never happy about me associating with the likes of Anthony Kelly and Paul Crawford, so you can be certain political opponents would use that against me.

I think that if I ran for public office, there are people who would do everything in their power to ruin my credibility and destroy my name. I have to decide whether I am willing to take that risk and whether it will benefit Changing Lives.

I would want answers as to why the Regeneration people have spent €150 million and yet we seem to have nothing to show for it. They claim that it is a long-term plan and it will be worth the wait, but people need to live their lives in the here and now. We need to foster a community spirit and bring back some pride in the area. That pride cannot be manufactured; it has to be nurtured and developed. We need to start with some small success stories.

Much of the work of Changing Lives is going to be about changing mindsets. We need to give people who have been let down by society a feeling of self worth and a feeling of belonging. If we can show these people who are being lost to drugs and crime that they are important, then they will get some real self-confidence and not the false bravado of a few lines of cocaine or six pints of strong lager.

If Changing Lives can be a catalyst for this, then the gangs will lose their stranglehold on the community and my life and all of our lives will be an awful lot safer as a result.

❖   ❖   ❖

TEN

BACK TO LIFE

J ust after 6 a.m. on 22 February 2010, thirty-five-year-old Daniel Treacy was delivering bread from his family's bakery to the Topaz petrol station on the Ennis Road in Limerick. Daniel's routine was like clockwork and this was one of his first stops every morning. He was just inside the door of the shop when an unmasked gunman approached him and shot him a number of times in the chest and head, killing him instantly.

Daniel had no involvement in gangland activity but his uncle was the notorious criminal Kieran Keane, who was killed by the McCarthy/ Dundon gang. Daniel Treacy's brother Owen was a key figure in Kieran Keane's gang and he gave evidence at Keane's murder trial. Owen was the prosecution's main witness as he had survived the murderous assault despite being stabbed seventeen times during the attack in January 2003. The gang left Owen for dead after luring him and Keane into an ambush. He was responsible for the jailing of Dessie Dundon, Anthony 'Noddy' McCarthy, David 'Frog Eyes' Stanners, Christopher 'Smokie' Costelloe and James McCarthy.

Owen agreed to testify on the condition that his father, Philly, was granted garda protection.

I met Philly Treacy a few weeks before Christmas 2011 and he told me that the gardaí had pulled his security. He said a senior officer had contacted him and told him that his protection detail was being removed.

A few days later my father received a similar phone call and was told the protection he received while he was working on his market stall was being withdrawn. Instead of having two armed detectives stationed at the Milk Market, they were going to send some unarmed uniformed officers instead.

For a couple of days I drove around behind Philly Treacy while he went on his bread round. That way my protection detail would follow close behind us and he would be safe. I'm sure the senior gardaí weren't pleased when they heard about what I had been doing, but I had no doubt that Philly was still a target.

The gangs have proven in the past that they are willing to wait years before striking and taking revenge. They waited three years to exact retribution for the murder of Eddie Ryan in the Moose Bar. The McCarthy/Dundons took a further seven years before striking out at Daniel Treacy. When he was being led away to start his prison sentence 'Noddy' McCarthy warned: 'For every action there's a reaction. Remember that.'

My relationship with the gardaí was becoming more strained as time went on. The level of contact I had with the senior officers had reduced dramatically and I felt that after the trial I was seen as an inconvenience. Despite this, and despite the fact that they had removed the protection from Philly and my father, I didn't really expect that they would leave me exposed.

On Monday, 19 December 2011 my liaison officer called me into Henry Street garda station for a meeting. This time there was no senior brass present. He told me quite succinctly that the threat against my person was now assessed as being 'moderate' and no longer warranted garda protection. I couldn't quite believe what I was hearing. After everything I had done for the State they were cutting me loose.

I wanted more information. How exactly had they assessed the risk? What intelligence did they have that suggested I was safe from the gang? But they refused to tell me anything.

My liaison officer said that some arrangements would be put in place, such as regular garda patrols through Carew Park. That sounds like something that should be happening in the normal course of events, rather than a special arrangement. They refused to give me their decision in writing, so there is no written evidence that could be used in a court case. More to the point, it would be very embarrassing if my family had a piece of paper saying there was a 'moderate' risk to my life and I ended up in a ditch, riddled with bullets.

I managed to secure a second meeting and I brought my solicitor with me this time. The gardaí were not happy with this. As soon as my solicitor introduced himself, a senior officer said there would be no meeting as there was nothing to discuss. He said the decision had been made and there was no going back on it. My solicitor said it was completely unacceptable for me to be treated in that manner and that I had legitimate concerns that they should address. The next trick the officers tried to pull was to tell us that they couldn't discuss anything concerning a witness with a solicitor. They said this was garda policy and that they would only talk to me.

Eventually they relented and brought us into a meeting room. We were told that my security risk was so minor that it was not of a level that even requires notification. Additionally the gardaí said they had serious problems with who I talk to. They said I was speaking with criminals and that this was unacceptable. I told them that I spoke with these people about football and that I was trying to do something positive in Southill by bringing the community together. I already knew senior officers didn't like me associating with Anthony Kelly and Paul Crawford because of their links to crime. I believe both men have turned their back on gangland and are trying to give something back to the community. They should not be condemned for the rest of their days. I would love to see other members of criminal gangs in Limerick do the same. The gardaí should be supporting the work we are doing, not trying to throw obstacles in our way.

But they knew all about my work with Hill Celtic and Changing Lives – it didn't matter what I was trying to do.

This new attitude was completely different from the one they had shown when they needed my help to get the gang members jailed. Back then they said it was almost inevitable that I was going to die violently if I did not come forward and make a statement. My evidence was so good that seven gang members pleaded guilty and ended up behind bars. In return the gardaí promised to protect me.

I would like to know hand on heart whether they actually believe I am under no threat or if it is down to budget cuts. I had to stand in front of a court of law and answer questions honestly and I would like the State to show me the same consideration. I realise that the public sector has been forced to cut back in many areas, but I feel it is wrong for the State to expect a man to testify against dangerous criminals and then remove his security when they have extracted everything they need.

My protection detail was withdrawn from midnight on 22 December. None of my family could believe that this was happening. My mother was particularly upset because she had asked me to step up and testify against the gang in the first place.

What made the news particularly hard to take was that we had been looking forward to a 'normal' Christmas at home with the family. Our preparations were already well under way. Gina and I had even travelled to Cork to do the Christmas shopping. In Limerick everyone knows who I am, and I feel a bit uncomfortable walking around the shops. It was great being able to behave almost like a normal couple again, buying gifts and food for Christmas. We weren't planning anything over the top or excessive: we just wanted a normal family celebration like hundreds of thousands of other families across the country.

There would never be a good time to lose the protection, but three days before Christmas seemed cruel and unnecessary. Of course by 22 December the courts were on holidays and it would have been difficult, if not impossible, to secure an injunction to prevent the decision from being acted upon, even if I could afford to go to court. It felt as if someone was deliberately trying to ruin our Christmas.

I spent almost a year looking over my shoulder for a gunman before the protection had been put in place. I was not relishing the prospect of having to go back to that. It had at least allowed me to have some semblance of a life, despite all the inconvenience.

In October 2011 I started going to the gym and trying to get fit again. I was losing weight and working hard, and seeing the results improved my mood and my self-esteem. I was starting to look forward to the future and Gina and I were beginning to plan ahead and enjoy family life again. My work with Hill Celtic and Changing Lives provided me with something to focus on. I was motivated and I had goals for the first time since the club closed. I was finally rebuilding my life after the threats, the intimidation and the trial. Things were improving until the gardaí dropped their bombshell.

Don't get me wrong: living under garda protection isn't something I would wish on my worst enemy, but if you really need it, living without it provokes massive stress and anxiety. If I am out driving I have to keep an eye on every single other vehicle on the road. I am hyper-vigilant when I approach traffic lights or junctions. I never want to be in a position where I'm blocked in. I always leave plenty of room between the jeep and the car in front so I can swing out and power away from a potential ambush. I haven't started wearing my bulletproof vest yet but it's only a matter of time.

On the evening of 31 Janurary 2012 my father received a phone call from the lad who was working on his rubbish-collection lorry on Hyde Road in Weston, just 100 metres away from where the Dundons live. The lorry had been petrol bombed while he was collecting rubbish from a house and he returned to find it in flames. The cab was burnt out and the vehicle was a write-off. I think the threat to my family and me is still very real and present.

I don't see how the gardaí can expect witnesses

to come forward in the future. If they see how other witnesses and their families have been treated, why would anyone believe the gardaí's promises?

I know that Steve Collins still has his protection and I have absolutely no problem with that. He lost his son Roy and he needs the protection. It shouldn't be an either/or situation. If the gang still presents a threat to one of their victims, then they are a threat to us all.

This gang has shown in the past that they will go after the easiest possible target. The murder of Daniel Treacy illustrates that they are happy to kill an innocent family member when they cannot get their number one target.

Limerick has been relatively quiet since my trial and there would be no one happier than me if that remains the situation. The split in McCarthy/Dundon gang means that they are turning on themselves at the moment. This might mean they are too worried about internal issues to come after me. But I find it very difficult to accept that not a single member of the gang has me on his hit list.

The more I learn about gangland, the less secure I feel. Some might think I am being paranoid, but that day in February 2010 when they tried to kidnap me outside Garryowen post office showed that the threat is very real. If I had not been on high alert that day

I might not be alive. Having to return to such a state of alertness after more than a year is soul destroying.

What little normality I had in my life has been taken away from me. I changed my mobile phone number again, after I heard an echo on my phone one day. I wasn't sure if someone was listening in to my calls or not, but I couldn't take the chance. One slip-up could lead to my death.

I feel like someone senior in the gardaí or the government has decided to play lotto with my life. They are taking a gamble with my safety and that of my family.

❖ ❖ ❖

Within days of the gardaí pulling their protection, several summonses for road traffic offences landed on the doormat. The gardaí have decided to prosecute me for parking offences, after they specifically instructed me to park my car close to my destination and not to leave it unattended for any length of time. I think it is vindictive of them to prosecute me for following the safety advice they gave me in the first place. I don't believe that I am above the law, but when the gardaí tell you to act in a certain manner to guarantee your own safety, you are bound to follow that advice. And why choose now to prosecute me?

Gina and I went away with the kids for a week in January 2012 to try and figure out what we were going to do. We didn't tell anyone outside the family where we were going because my security antennae were back working overtime. Getting out of the country was the only way we could reduce our stress levels and try to look at things from a distance and see the big picture. It was such a relief for us to be able to walk along the street like a normal family.

It gave me time to think about the future and how we were going to live. We also had to decide whether we were going to remain in Limerick. I decided that I am not going to let these latest disappointments interfere with my plans for the future. I'm going to stay in Limerick and make Hill Celtic and Changing Lives a success. I want to stay here and be part of something that makes Limerick better.

As soon as we got back from holiday, I had to appear in court again. This time I was accused of obstructing the back of my neighbour's house as I loaded my jeep with camping equipment for a weekend away with the family.

I had to walk into Limerick District Court with every criminal in the city or else a bench warrant would be issued for my immediate arrest. I was ordered to attend court at 10.30 a.m. on 25 January, but by lunchtime my case had not been heard. That meant that anybody who saw me in the courthouse knew I'd have to return after lunch, giving them plenty of time to arrange a hit.

When the case was eventually called, my solicitor asked for CCTV evidence and statements from the gardaí. The gardaí suddenly dropped the charges.

It was depressing to see all the youngsters in front of the judge that day, facing charges for possession of small amounts of cannabis. They were now in the system; their downward spiral into criminality had begun. Those guys are likely to become regular fixtures at the courts unless someone can intervene and steer them in the right direction. Our political leaders are failing these lads. Scooping them up and bringing them before the judge to fine them €200 is not going to stop them from reoffending. It doesn't act as a deterrent and it doesn't address the issues that made them take drugs in the first place. All it does is put a black mark against their name, label them and place them firmly on the gardaí's radar.

I know Changing Lives has a role in helping these kids. But the system has to change how it deals with them too. To effect change like that you need political power. It seems that if I want to help myself and others I will have to look seriously at running for political office. There is no point in me sitting on the sidelines and complaining, when I could be trying to change the situation.

❖ ❖ ❖

Looking back at everything I have been through, I don't know whether the sacrifices have been worth it. I am supposed to believe that my life is no longer in danger but I cannot accept that I can safely drop my guard. Whenever somebody has taken a stand against the gangs, it has led to another murder; either they are hit or someone close to them is targeted. I would be the happiest man in the world if the guards were right and the risk to me was minimal. But I just don't believe it.

If I received another threat, I'm not sure I would report it. I have had enough of the criminal justice system, and assisting the gardaí left me worse off in the end. My ordeal has completely destroyed my faith in the authorities. The victim is a pawn on their chessboard, and once you've helped capture the opposing king you are left exposed.

All the gang members will be back on the streets within the next couple of years, so that is something

I am going to have to deal with. The gang culture in Limerick has to be tackled before the McCarthy/ Dundons are back on the streets, taking control of youngsters and striking fear into people's lives again.

The future is difficult to predict. Nobody will ever be able to convince me that there is no longer a threat against my safety. I trust nobody except my family and those closest to me. I'm convinced there is a bullet out there with my name on it, and that is why I will be looking over my shoulder for the rest of my days.

❖ ❖ ❖